FLUTE FOR EVERYONE

Learn Flute in 60 Days (COURSE 1)

Indian Classical Flute / Bansuri / Bamboo Flute

Notation Approved By Guruji: Sri D. Madhusudan

SECOND EDITION

Riddhi Sanyal

Notations of ***Prelims, Songs & Ragas*** are available in ***Indian Convention & Sheet Music***. Kindle Edition Contains ***Music Files***.

This book is available via

Paperback (B/W): pothi.com   **ISBN: 9789353915520**
Paperback (COLOR): amazon.com   **ISBN: 9781694935779**
EBook: All Marketplace of Amazon like Amazon.com, amazon.in, amazon.jp, amazon.uk and others.

Contents

Flute for everyone 1

1.0   Dedication 5

2.0   Preface 5

    After completing the course, you will be able to 5

3.0   How Flute Becomes Classical Instrument 7

4.0   Guidelines to Purchase Flute 8

    Beginners 8

    6 months to 1 year of learning 8

    3 years of learning 8

    5 years of learning 8

    Why scale matters 9

5.0   Indian Music Convention w.r.t. Western Notes 9

    Lower Octave with Flute playing position 9

    Middle Octave with Flute playing position 10

    Higher Octave with Flute playing position 10

6.0   The Making of Flute 11

7.0   Learner Section 1 | Begin with Flute & Play SARGAM 12

    Day 1 – Holding Flute and Making sound 12

    Blowing Technique and position of the flute 12

    Playing Default Sound - Tibra Ma, Notation Symbol = M, Western: F# w.r.t. C scale 13

    Day 2, Day 3 – Play m, G, R, S 14

    Playing ma, Notation Symbol = m, Western: F w.r.t. C scale 14

    Playing Ga, Notation Symbol = G, Western: E w.r.t. C Scale 15

    Playing Re, Notation Symbol = R, Western: D w.r.t. C Scale 16

    Playing Sa, Notation Symbol = C, Western: C w.r.t. C Scale 17

    Day 4, Day 5 – Play Pa, Dha, Ni, Sa of Middle Octave 17

    Playing Pa, Notation Symbol = P, Western: G w.r.t. C Scale 18

    Playing Dha, Notation Symbol = D, Western: A w.r.t. C Scale 19

    Playing Ni, Notation Symbol = N, Western: B w.r.t. C Scale 19

    Playing Sa', Notation Symbol = Ŝ, Western: C6 w.r.t. C5 Scale 20

    Day 6, Day 7 – Play entire Middle Octave 21

    Day 8 – Learn Lower octave notes 21

Playing Ni, Notation Symbol = N, Western: B4 w.r.t. C5 Scale 21
Playing Dha, Notation Symbol = D, Western: A4 w.r.t. C5 Scale 21
Playing Pa, Notation Symbol = P, Western: G4 w.r.t. C5 Scale 22

Day 9 – Learn higher octave notes 22

Playing Re', Notation Symbol = R̂, Western: D6 w.r.t. C6 Scale 22
Playing Ga', Notation Symbol = Ĝ, Western: E6 w.r.t. C5 Scale 23
Playing ma', Notation Symbol = ṁ, Western: F6 w.r.t. C5 scale 23

8.0   Learner Section 2 | Preliminary Practices Flute 24

Day 10, Day 11 – Play 2 notes at a time 24

Exercise 1: Play 2 same notes at a time 24
Exercise 2: Play 2 sequential notes at a time 25

Day 12 - Play alternate notes 27
Day 13, Day 14 – Learn to play with 8 Beat (4+4) Taal 29
Day 15 – Learn Rest / Gap 30
Day 16 – Learn ½ Notes and ½ Rests 32
Day 17, 18, 19 – Recap with more Exercises 33
Day 20 – Progression on 3 notes at a time 35
Day 21 - Progression on 4 notes at a time 36
Day 23 – Learn to play with 6 Beat (3+3) Taal – Dadra 37
Day 24, Day 25 – Revision & Practice lessons with Sargam 38

9.0   Learner Section 3 | Play Music & Songs in Flute 41

Day 26 – Play Simple tune – Happy Birthday 41

Playing Komal (Flat) ni, Notation Symbol = n, Western: Bb w.r.t. C Scale ... 41

Day 27 – Play Simple tune – 'Twinkle Twinkle' 42
Day 28 – Play 'We Shall Overcome' 43
Day 29 – Play 'Jamaican Farewell' 44
Day 30 – Play 'Do A Deer' from Sound of Music 46
Day 31 – Play Scottish tune 'Auld Lang Syne' 49
Day 32 – Play simple Hindi Song – A Chal Ke Tujhe 51
Day 33 – Play simple Rabindra Sangeet – Phule Phule 53
Day 34 – Play Hindi Bhajan – Om Jai Jagadish Hare 55
Day 35, Day 36, Day 37 – Revision & Further Lessons 57

10.0   Learner Section 4 | Play Indian Classical Ragas 60

Day 38 to Day 42 – Raga Hansadhwani 60
Day 43 to Day 46 – Raga Durga 66

RIDDHI SANYAL

Day 47 to Day 50 – Raga Bilaval...72
Day 51 to Day 54 – Raga Mand 75
Day 55 to Day 59 – Raga Bhupali (also known as Bhopali / Bhoopali) 80
Day 60 – Recap, Further learning steps 85

11.0   Image Gallery...86
12.0   Improvisation of Classical Flute to 8 Hole 92
13.0   Instrumental Workshop & Recent Performances 95

2017 March, Varanasi, Musical Gathering...95
2017 Aug, Bangalore: Musical Workshop, Street Performance & Organized Grand
Function: 96

14.0   Flute and Meditation 100
15.0   About Guruji, Musical Maestro Sri D. Madhusudan............................ 103

Guruji's life and Guru Lineages 103
My First visit to Guruji.. 103
Musical Experience of Guruji in various instruments................................... 104

String Instruments: 104
Bowing Instrument:.. 104

16.0   Appendix 106
17.0   Index.. 107

Figures.. 107
Tables 107
Exercises 108
Sheet Music... 109

18.0   References 110
19.0   About the Author 111
20.0   Feedback & Contacts.. 112

Email: Riddhi.Sanyal@gmail.com 112
Phone Number: +91 9051653871.. 112
WhatsApp: https://wa.me/919051653871... 112
YouTube Channel: https://www.youtube.com/c/MusicalJourneys 112
Instagram: https://www.instagram.com/riddhi.sanyal/................................. 112
Facebook Profile: https://www.facebook.com/riddhi.sanyal.12..................... 112
Author Page: https://www.amazon.com/author/riddhi................................. 112

RIDDHI SANYAL

1.0   Dedication

➢ Swami Sadhanananda Giri Maharaj
➢ MAA, BABA, Priyanka, Pragyan and all Family Members to bless & support me in music
➢ Musical Maestro, Guruji Sri Madhusudan Das

2.0   Preface

Primary objective of this book is to illustrate how to play, how to begin with Indian Classical Flute / Bansuri. After going through the chapters and exercises, you will gradually understand the basics and you will get a definitive guideline with next steps. **Notations are created in both Indian convention and sheet music considering in mind that anyone from anywhere in the world can start learning Flute, play songs and learn Indian Classical Music.**

Bansuri / Indian Bamboo Flute is one of the finest Hindustani classical instrument nowadays. This book contains a little background on the evolution of the Flute as classical music, making of flute, guideline to purchase and in-depth lessons of your journey as a Flute Player. At the end, book covers the real story of Musical workshops, Innovations and Flute & Meditation. This book will be handy for everyone who loves Flute. The lessons of Flute are given day-to-day basis so that you can effectively learn within 60 days from the Purchase of your Flute. After completing the exercise with sincere practice, you can quantify your learning and will be ready to start practice Ragas in Indian Classical Music. The Learning lessons are designed with most scientific way for the beginner or anyone who loves flute. To make the learning effective and measurable, Indian notation & Sheet Music are supported by beats / *Taal*, Gaps, repeat instructions and further steps.

After completing the course, you will be able to

- Hold and play the flute
- Play notes in Rhythm or Taal – 6 beat, 8 beat, 16 beat
- Read and play notation and play world famous songs.
- Read Sheet Music and Indian Notation
- Play 5 Ragas in Flute in 16 beat - Tintaal

Section of Hindi Famous Song 'A Chal Ke Tujhe' is given below to quickly glance the simplicity of the notation in Indian Convention.

RIDDHI SANYAL

Time Sig	1	2	3	4	5	6	7	8	Times to play	Return to Time Sig
①	–	–	–	–	–	–	–	P		
②	(S	SR	S	P	S	SR	S	P		
③	S	SR	G	mG	mG	R	–	P		
④	R	RG	R	P	R	RG	R	SR	2	
⑤	N	NS	P	Pm	G	–	–	P		
⑥	S	SR	G	mG	S	–	–	) (G		② – 1

Similarly, the starting section of famous song 'Do A Deer' is shown below to share the famous world music in simplified Sheet music to comfortably play in Flute.

Do A Deer, A Female Deer

- Simplified for Flute, by Riddhi Sanyal

"Music is an agreeable harmony for the honor of God and the permissible delights of the soul." — Johann Sebastian Bach

RIDDHI SANYAL

3.0   How Flute Becomes Classical Instrument

Since ancient times we have observed flute playing in India. Lord Krishna has played flute at *Vrindavan*[1] 5000 years ago. Flute was often observed in the cowherd's hand to orchestrate and to bring the animals back to home during the evening.

During 19th century, **Fakir Aftabuddin Khan**, elder brother of Baba Allauddin Khan Saheb[2], was one of the greatest Flutist in India. However, he dedicated the Music on God and did not wanted any fame. So there is no recordings of his playing.

Credit goes to **Pt. Pannalal Ghosh** to convert Flute from the hand of cowherds into a classical musical instrument. During the early 20th century, he has invented the bigger Flutes where any classical raga can be practiced. It's a nice story behind this. Little Pannalal started his learnings from his father Sri Akshay Kumar Ghosh who was a *Sitarist*[3]. Pannalal has a strong learning determination to learn Flute and he was practicing his Sitar lessons on the flutes received from cowherds.

During his early childhood, Pannalal Ghosh's family lived near a river named *Kirtankhola*. While taking bath in the river, he got a long walking stick made of Bamboo. The Bamboo stick was longer than the traditional cowherd flutes. That stick contains few holes and Pannalal tried to play the long stick and realize that Ragas can be played better in longer flutes than the smaller one. Then in the journey, he has invented 6-hole base flutes, which is suitable for Classical Ragas to learn or practice.

Later on **Pt Hariprasad Chaurasia** has popularize the Indian Bamboo Flute to the entire world with unique style of playing the Indian classical music. He has applied nice techniques to beautify the sound and rhythm in Flute playing.

---

[1] *Vrindavan is a sacred place at UP, India; nearer to Sri Krishna's birthplace. It is in Mahabharata that, Lord Krishna spent first 11-12 years of Childhood days at Vrindavan.*

[2] *Baba Alauddin Khan Sahib has reformed Indian Classical ragas on early 20th Century. He is the Guru of legendary son Ali Akbar Khan, daughter Annapurna Devi, Pt. Ravi Shankar, Pt. Nikhil Banerjee, Pt. Pannalal Ghosh & others.*

[3] *Sitarist is the musician who plays the instrument Sitar*

RIDDHI SANYAL

4.0   Guidelines to Purchase Flute

Beginners

If you know a little basic before your first flute purchase, it will be easier to check and find the ideal flute for you from store.

Thumb rules are your fingers should be able to cover the 6-holes properly. Three fingers from both hands - index, middle, and ring fingers are used to play 6-hole flute, however thumb and little finger support the flute at correct position. Please check, whether your fingers are able to cover the holes completely and there is no leakage when you are blowing.

Quality of the sound depends how you are blowing. Before selection, you should check whether you are able to make sound comfortably. Easier you can make sound; it is more suitable with your blowing pattern. Everyone will blow in a different pattern and the same flute can sound little different with others than yours.

For the beginner, it's recommended to use higher frequency flutes (smaller flutes). Once stable sound comes and student gains control, he or she can choose lower frequency flute. **Therefore, there is no need to purchase multiple flutes at a time.** Only go for the one, which you really need now.

- ✓   For the children of age range 5 - 10 years, its recommended to start with smaller flutes of scale **higher D, D#, E** during the initial days.
- ✓   Students of age range 10 – 15, can start with the **higher scale C#, D**.
- ✓   Rest of age range & adults can start with higher scales from **C, C#, D** whichever suites the finger and sound quality.

There is no age barrier to start with. We have observed students who started at the age of 60 and after practicing for 5-6 years, he has started teaching.

6 months to 1 year of learning

Down the line 6 months to 1 year of continuous learning, if you are comfortable with beginner flute, you can get little lower frequency flute. For example, if you have started with higher D# / E, you can take C. If anyone has started with higher scales C, C# or D, can take A scaled flute.

3 years of learning

If you are a sincere learner and completed 3 years of learning course, then it's recommended for you to take little lower frequency flute, for example **G**.

5 years of learning

Once you complete 5 years, your target will be to take the base **E flute**. Always remember that Gurudeb recommended his students to play E scale flutes for practicing classical music. His suggestion was not to go further down below base E scale flute.

RIDDHI SANYAL

Why scale matters

Now you can understand why a flutist generally have so many flutes. Not really, the reason for carrying different scaled flutes are to tune with vocal scale or to the scale of other instruments. Human vocal scales are generally Bb for female and C/C# for male voice. Different instruments have different natural scales, Ex Violin - D, Mandolin - D, Sarod - B, Ukulele - C etc. Flute is not an instrument where you can change scale. Therefore, you have to carry multiple scale flutes to play with other musicians in a concert.

5.0   Indian Music Convention w.r.t. Western Notes

Greatest poet & composer Gurudeb *Sri Rabindranath Tagore* depicted his songs in Indian Notation (called *Swaralipi*) since 1880. During early 20th century, ***Pt. Vishnu Narayan Bhatkhande*** reformed the Indian Notation. In our exercises, we will follow the notations from *Pt Bhatkhande Ji*.

Table 1,2,3 contains the Indian Notation Symbols & conversion to western scale. All possible notes of flute are given and their corresponding western note is given. Consider the scale of flute is C.

Lower Octave[4] with Flute playing position

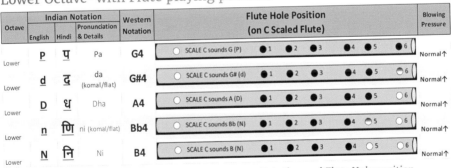

Table 1: Lower Octave - Indian Notation, Western Notation and Flute Hole position

---

[4] *Octave (in Hindi, Saptak) consists of 7 consecutive Major notes. If you start from C scale, the octave will contain the notes CDEFGAB. Bansuri / Flute supports the range of playing portion of lower octave, complete middle octave and portion of higher octave.*

RIDDHI SANYAL

Middle Octave with Flute playing position

Octave	Indian Notation			Western Notation	Flute Hole Position (on C Scaled Flute)	Blowing Pressure
	English	Hindi	Pronunciation & Details			
Middle	S	सा	Sa	C5	SCALE C sounds C (S) ●1 ●2 ●3 ○4 ○5 ○6	Normal ↑
Middle	r	ऋ	Ri (komal/flat)	C#5	SCALE C sounds C# (r) ●1 ●2 ○3 ○4 ○5 ○6	Normal ↑
Middle	R	र	Re	D5	SCALE C sounds D (R) ●1 ●2 ○3 ○4 ○5 ○6	Normal ↑
Middle	g	ज्ञ	gya (komal/flat)	D#5	SCALE C sounds D# (g) ●1 ○2 ○3 ○4 ○5 ○6	Normal ↑
Middle	G	ग	Ga	E5	SCALE C sounds E (G) ●1 ○2 ○3 ○4 ○5 ○6	Normal ↑
Middle	m	म	ma	F5	SCALE C sounds F (m) ○1 ○2 ○3 ○4 ○5 ○6	Normal ↑
Middle	M	क्ष	Ma (tibra/sharp)	F#5	SCALE C sounds F# (M) ○1 ○2 ○3 ○4 ○5 ○6	Normal ↑
Middle	P	प	Pa	G5	SCALE C sounds G (P) ●1 ●2 ●3 ●4 ●5 ●6	High ↑↑
Middle	d	द	da (komal/flat)	G#5	SCALE C sounds G# (d) ●1 ●2 ●3 ●4 ●5 ○6	High ↑↑
Middle	D	ध	Dha	A5	SCALE C sounds A (D) ●1 ●2 ●3 ●4 ●5 ○6	High ↑↑
Middle	n	णि	ni (komal/flat)	Bb5	SCALE C sounds Bb (N) ●1 ●2 ●3 ●4 ○5 ○6	High ↑↑
Middle	N	नि	Ni	B5	SCALE C sounds B (N) ●1 ●2 ●3 ●4 ○5 ○6	High ↑↑

Table 2: Middle Octave - Indian Notation, Western Notation and Flute Hole position

Higher Octave with Flute playing position

Octave	Indian Notation			Western Notation	Flute Hole Position (on C Scaled Flute)	Blowing Pressure
	English	Hindi	Pronunciation & Details			
Higher	Ŝ	सां	Sa	C6	SCALE C sounds C (S) ●1 ●2 ●3 ○4 ○5 ○6	High ↑↑
Higher	r̂	ऋं	Ri (komal/flat)	C#6	SCALE C sounds C# (r) ●1 ●2 ○3 ○4 ○5 ○6	High ↑↑
Higher	R̂	रं	Re	D6	SCALE C sounds D (R) ●1 ●2 ○3 ○4 ○5 ○6	High ↑↑
Higher	ĝ	ज्ञं	gya (komal/flat)	D#6	SCALE C sounds D# (g) ●1 ○2 ○3 ○4 ○5 ○6	High ↑↑
Higher	Ĝ	गं	Ga	E6	SCALE C sounds E (G) ●1 ○2 ○3 ○4 ○5 ○6	High ↑↑
Higher	ṁ	मं	ma	F6	SCALE C sounds F (m) ○1 ○2 ○3 ○4 ○5 ○6	High ↑↑
Higher	Ḿ	क्षं	Ma (tibra/sharp)	F#6	SCALE C sounds F# (M) ○1 ○2 ○3 ○4 ○5 ○6	High ↑↑

Table 3: Higher Octave - Indian Notation, Western Notation and Flute Hole position

> "The most exciting rhythms seem unexpected and complex, the most beautiful melodies simple and inevitable." — W.H. Auden

RIDDHI SANYAL

6.0   The Making of Flute

To make Indian Bamboo Flute of 6-hole, these are the steps followed by our Guruji **Sri D. Madhusudan**. Steps are shared here to everyone to have a feel on the effort required to produce one professional quality Flute.

1. Need to purchase the good quality Bamboo from Tripura, Assam, UP and North-East Indian areas.
2. Bamboo must be having **equal diameters at both sides**.
3. Bamboo with both side hollow, is good to start with. If the Bamboo is one side blocked, then the measurements are aligned accordingly.
4. Bamboo should be seasoned with hot & cold water.
5. **Forging step:** Hot Burning Red Iron round stick is needed to make the holes. You have to be extremely careful to avoid cracks of Bamboo during Forging.
6. **Measurement:** First, the blowing hole has to be created.
7. Then comparing the **Air volume with water / sand**, need to mark the holes accordingly.
8. After completing & again, the flute should be seasoned.
9. Finally, **fine tuning** with cutting tool-sets to make the hole larger and tune with correct frequency.
10. Block the open side beside the mouth whole with a round rubber / cork. This is not applicable to one side blocked Bamboo.
11. If the frequency is little lesser than desired scale, it's okay to pick that. More you play; the frequency of the Flute goes up by 1/4 to 1/2 scale.
12. **It's very difficult to arrive a Flute in correct frequency / scale like C, Bb, C# or Base E scale. After 3–4 flutes, one will be created in perfect scale.**
13. Remember: Every 2–3 Bamboo will produce one **good quality Flute**; every 3–4 Flutes will produce one finest quality **perfect Scaled Flute**.
14. Key thing is the **Measurement**. That tunes the flute to Hindustani Classical tuning or like Western tuning. Only masters can tune a Flute correctly.

RIDDHI SANYAL

7.0   Learner Section 1 | Begin with Flute & Play SARGAM[5]

Day 1 – Holding Flute and Making sound

Hold the flute as shown in the below Figure 1. Left thumb will be stretched underneath the flute. Try to produce sound with all holes open. This step may take a day to 7 days. Figure 1 shows the way to hold the flute for a right-handed person.

Blowing Technique and position of the flute

- ✓ Take a deep breath and blow gently in a steady pace
- ✓ **Portion of lower lip should touch the blowing hole**. Try to cover 30% of the blowing hole with your lower lip.
- ✓ Slightly rotate the flute on playing and fix it at the position with maximum sound with minimum blowing effort.
- ✓ Not to blow too hard. With more pressure, a noisy / high frequency sound will produce initially. Control your breath and blow steadily to avoid that sound.
- ✓ Try to avoid the loss of air from your mouth going outside the blowing hole. That will improve your efficiency of playing.

---

[5] *Sargam – Word is originated from the first 4 notes of SRGmPDNŜ. It is the musical combination of the notes. Ex: SG RS Gm PN Ŝ NŜ NP mG RS*

RIDDHI SANYAL

Playing Default Sound – Tibra Ma, Notation Symbol = M, Western: F# w.r.t. C scale

All open hole sound of a flute is ***Tibra*[6] Ma (M)**. Try to follow the guidelines on making sound out of any flute.

✓   Stable sound can be played with consistency on blowing pressure
✓   Before exhaling complete breath, take a deep breath and play again. That will not change the frequency of your current note.
✓   Try to play at least 3 – 5 seconds at a stretch of breath. Sustaining for more time will help you to create stable sound.

○ SCALE C sounds F# (M)   ○ 1   ○ 2   ○ 3   ○ 4   ○ 5   ○ 6

Figure 1: Default Flute sound. Tibra Ma - Notation symbol M. (F# w.r.t. C Scale)

---

[6] *The term Tibra means sharp. So Tibra Ma reflects to F# on the scale of C.*

RIDDHI SANYAL

Day 2, Day 3 – Play m, G, R, S

Playing ma, Notation Symbol = m, Western: F w.r.t. C scale

- ✓ To play normal / *Shuddha*[7] ma, block the first hole around 50 - 75% with Left Hand Index finger.
- ✓ Blowing pressure impacts the sound as well as flute rotation influences the sound person to person.
- ✓ Hence, the coverage of the first hole generally varies 50 - 75% for different person. Ex: if your pressure is more, then you need to block around 75% to produce **m**.

○ SCALE C sounds F (m) ● 1   ○ 2   ○ 3   ○ 4   ○ 5   ○ 6

Figure 2: Flute position - Ma - Notation symbol m. (F w.r.t. C Scale)

---

[7] Shuddha - The Major Notes, i.e., SRGmPDN are termed as Shuddha Swars. Corresponding western notes are CDEFGAB

RIDDHI SANYAL

Once you are comfortable playing ma, next steps will be to play cover one by one finger by left hand to cover the Ga, Re, Sa.

Playing Ga, Notation Symbol = G, Western: E w.r.t. C Scale

✓ Block the **first** hole fully with Left Hand Index finger.
✓ No leakage of air is important.
✓ Blowing pressure is normal.
✓ It may be required to play ma, Ga in the same breath initially.
✓ Once stable, practice ma and Ga in separate breath.

| ○ SCALE C sounds E (G) | ● 1 | ○ 2 | ○ 3 | ○ 4 | ○ 5 | ○ 6 |

Figure 3: Flute position - Ga - Notation symbol G. (E w.r.t. C Scale)

RIDDHI SANYAL

✓ Place the Left Hand Index finger to block the **first** hole completely.

✓ Keep the Left hand middle finger to block the **second** hole completely.

✓ No leakage of air is important.

✓ Blowing pressure is normal.

✓ It may be required to play ma, Ga, Re in the same breath initially. After stability, play each note in separate breath.

✓ Practice m G R, R G m... more and more to gain stability on each sound.

SCALE C sounds D (R)   ● 1   ● 2   ○ 3   ○ 4   ○ 5   ○ 6

Figure 4: Flute position - Re - Notation symbol R. (D w.r.t. C Scale)

RIDDHI SANYAL

Playing Sa, Notation Symbol = C, Western: C w.r.t. C Scale

- ✓ Place the Left Hand Index finger to block the **first** hole completely.
- ✓ Use Left hand middle finger to block the **second** hole completely.
- ✓ Keep Left hand Ring finger to block **third** hole completely.
- ✓ No leakage of air is important.
- ✓ Blowing pressure is normal.
- ✓ It may be required to play ma, Ga, Re, Sa in the same breath initially. After stability, play each note in separate breath.
- ✓ Practice m G R S, S R G m… more and more to gain stability on each sound.

| ○ SCALE C sounds C (S) | ● 1 | ● 2 | ● 3 | ○ 4 | ○ 5 | ○ 6 |

Figure 5: Flute position - Sa - Notation symbol S. (C w.r.t. C Scale)

Day 4, Day 5 – Play Pa, Dha, Ni, Sa of Middle Octave

Once you are comfortable on S R G m, please proceed with other notes P D N Ŝ.

RIDDHI SANYAL

Playing Pa, Notation Symbol = P, Western: G w.r.t. C Scale

Position of Pa is all holes blocked completely.
- ✓ Place the Left Hand Index finger to block the **first** hole completely.
- ✓ Use the Left hand middle finger to block the **second** hole completely.
- ✓ Use Left hand Ring finger to block **third** hole completely.
- ✓ Apply Right Hand index finger to block **fourth** Hole completely.
- ✓ Use Right Hand middle finger to block **fifth** Hole completely.
- ✓ Use Right Hand ring finger to block **sixth** Hole completely.
- ✓ No leakage of air is important.
- ✓ **Blowing pressure** is **higher** than until now you played.
- ✓ Practice P m G R S, S R G m P, ... more and more to gain stability on each sound.

Figure 6: Flute position - Pa - Notation symbol P. (G w.r.t. C Scale)

RIDDHI SANYAL

Playing Dha, Notation Symbol = D, Western: A w.r.t. C Scale

To play Dha, 1st to 5th holes should be blocked completely leaving 6th Hole open.
- ✓ Place the Left Hand Index finger to block the **first** hole completely.
- ✓ Use the Left hand middle finger to block the **second** hole completely.
- ✓ Use Left hand Ring finger to block **third** hole completely.
- ✓ Apply Right Hand index finger to block **fourth** Hole completely.
- ✓ Use Right Hand middle finger to block **fifth** Hole completely.
- ✓ No leakage of air is important.
- ✓ Blowing pressure is higher than normal.
- ✓ Practice D P m G R S, S R G m P D, ...

| ○ SCALE C sounds A (D) | ● 1 | ● 2 | ● 3 | ● 4 | ● 5 | ○ 6 |

Figure 7: Flute position - Dha - Notation symbol D. (A w.r.t. C Scale)

Playing Ni, Notation Symbol = N, Western: B w.r.t. C Scale

RIDDHI SANYAL

To play Ni, 1st to 4th holes should be blocked completely leaving 5th & 6th Holes open.

To play Ni, 1st to 4th holes should be blocked completely leaving 5th & 6th Holes open.
- ✓ Place the Left Hand Index finger to block the **first** hole completely.
- ✓ Use the Left hand middle finger to block the **second** hole completely.
- ✓ Use Left hand Ring finger to block **third** hole completely.
- ✓ Apply Right Hand index finger to block **fourth** Hole completely.
- ✓ No leakage of air is important.
- ✓ Blowing pressure is **higher** than normal.
- ✓ Practice N D P m G R S, S R G m P D N, …

Figure 8: Flute position - Ni - Notation symbol N. (B w.r.t. C Scale)

Playing Sa', Notation Symbol = Ŝ, Western: C6 w.r.t. C5 Scale

This is the higher octave Sa. Only difference to play is the higher blowing pressure.
- ✓ Place the Left Hand Index finger to block the **first** hole completely.
- ✓ Use the Left hand middle finger to block the **second** hole completely.
- ✓ Use Left hand Ring finger to block **third** hole completely.
- ✓ 4th, 5th and 6th holes should be in open position.
- ✓ No leakage of air is important.

RIDDHI SANYAL

- ✓ Blowing pressure is **higher** than normal.
- ✓ Practice Ŝ N D P m G R S, S R G m P D N Ŝ, ...

Figure 9: Flute position - Sa' - Notation symbol Ŝ. (C6 w.r.t. C5 Scale)

Further Guidance –
- ✓ In a Flute, Sa, Re, Ga, ma can be played with normal blowing force.
- ✓ Pa, Dha, Ni, Sa' can be played with higher than normal blowing force.
- ✓ One has to practice Sa, Re, Ga, ma, Pa, Dha, Ni, Sa' for initial few days to gain stability of each notes in a flute. More practice produces more stable sound.
- ✓ Sharp or Flat notes are taught gradually after 6 months to 1 year from beginning. For learner's interest on the flute position on each notes, all possible notes given already in the Table1, Table 2, Table3.

Day 6, Day 7 – Play entire Middle Octave

Key outcomes
- ✓ Play entire middle octave at upward and downward direction.
- ✓ Will be able to play with more stable sound

Further Playing Guidelines
- ✓ Take single note in single breath initially and try to play for as long as you can. For ex: Try each notes for 5 – 10 seconds.
- ✓ Always play each note for equal time signature / tempo.
- ✓ Once you are comfortable, you can increase the tempo.

Day 8 – Learn Lower octave notes

Playing Ni, Notation Symbol = N, Western: B4 w.r.t. C5 Scale

To play Ni, 1st to 4th holes should be blocked completely leaving 5th & 6th Holes open.
- ✓ Place the Left Hand Index finger to block the **first** hole completely.
- ✓ Use the Left hand middle finger to block the **second** hole completely.
- ✓ Use Left hand Ring finger to block **third** hole completely.
- ✓ Apply Right Hand index finger to block **fourth** Hole completely.
- ✓ No leakage of air is important.
- ✓ Blowing pressure is **normal**.
- ✓ Practice m G R S N, N S R G m, ...

Figure 10: Flute position - Ni - Notation symbol N. (B4 w.r.t. C5 Scale)

Playing Dha, Notation Symbol = D, Western: A4 w.r.t. C5 Scale

To play Dha, 1st to 5th holes should be blocked completely leaving 6th Hole open.
- ✓ Place the Left Hand Index finger to block the **first** hole completely.

RIDDHI SANYAL

- ✓ Use the Left hand middle finger to block the **second** hole completely.
- ✓ Use Left hand Ring finger to block **third** hole completely.
- ✓ Apply Right Hand index finger to block **fourth** Hole completely.
- ✓ Keep Right Hand middle finger to block **fifth** Hole completely.
- ✓ No leakage of air is important.
- ✓ Blowing pressure is **normal**.
- ✓ Practice S N̲ D̲, D̲ N̲ S, ...

Figure 11: Flute position - <u>Dha</u> - Notation symbol D̲. (A4 w.r.t. C5 Scale)

Playing Pa, Notation Symbol = P̲, Western: G4 w.r.t. C5 Scale

To play <u>Pa</u>, all holes should be blocked completely.
- ✓ Place the Left Hand Index finger to block the **first** hole completely.
- ✓ Use the Left hand middle finger to block the **second** hole completely.
- ✓ Use Left hand Ring finger to block **third** hole completely.
- ✓ Apply Right Hand index finger to block **fourth** Hole completely.
- ✓ Use Right Hand middle finger to block **fifth** Hole completely.
- ✓ Use Right Hand ring finger to block **sixth** Hole completely.
- ✓ No leakage of air is important.
- ✓ Blowing pressure is **normal** or **lesser**.
- ✓ Practice S N̲ D̲ P̲, P̲ D̲ N̲ S, ...

Figure 12: Flute position - <u>Pa</u> - Notation symbol P̲. (G4 w.r.t. C5 Scale)

Day 9 – Learn higher octave notes

We have already learned to play the Sa' (C6). It's time to learn the rest of the notes in the higher octave.

Playing Re', Notation Symbol = R̂, Western: D6 w.r.t. C6 Scale

- ✓ We have already learned the normal R (Re / D5). Only difference is to blow with **higher** pressure to produce R̂ (Re' / D6).
- ✓ Practice Ŝ R̂, N Ŝ R̂... more and more to gain stability on each sound.

Figure 13: Flute position – Re' - Notation symbol R̂. (D6 w.r.t. C6 Scale)

Playing Ga', Notation Symbol = Ĝ, Western: E6 w.r.t. C5 Scale

✓ Only technique difference between normal G and higher Ĝ is to blow with **higher** pressure with the same finger position.

✓ Once stable, practice Ŝ Ȓ Ĝ, Ĝ Ȓ Ŝ... N Ŝ Ȓ Ĝ, Ĝ Ȓ Ŝ N

| ○ SCALE C5 sounds E6 (Ĝ) | ● 1 | ○ 2 | ○ 3 | ○ 4 | ○ 5 | ○ 6 |

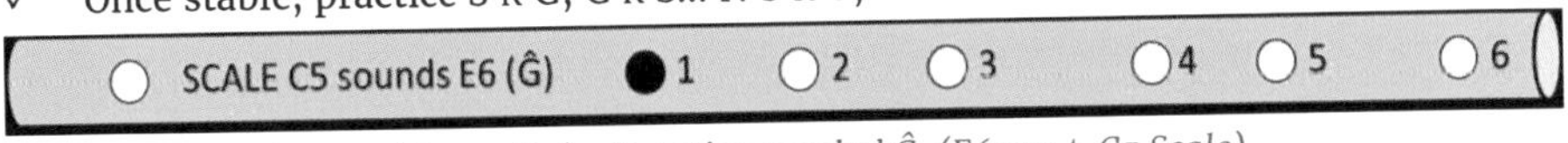

Figure 14: Flute position – Ga' - Notation symbol Ĝ. (E6 w.r.t. C5 Scale)

Playing ma', Notation Symbol = ṁ, Western: F6 w.r.t. C5 scale

✓ Playing with **more blowing pressure** on the position of normal ma will produce higher octave ma (ṁ).

✓ Hole coverage varies on the blowing pressure & flute position. Generally, its 50 – 75% covered for most of the persons.

✓ Practice the below to gain more control on the higher octave notes.
  ○ Ĝ ṁ, ṁ Ĝ
  ○ Ȓ Ĝ ṁ, ṁ Ĝ Ȓ
  ○ Ŝ Ȓ Ĝ ṁ, ṁ Ĝ Ȓ Ŝ

| ○ SCALE C5 sounds F6 (ṁ) | ◑ 1 | ○ 2 | ○ 3 | ○ 4 | ○ 5 | ○ 6 |

Figure 15: Flute position - Ma' - Notation symbol ṁ. (F6 w.r.t. C5 Scale)

▌ *"Music fills the infinite between two souls" — Rabindranath Tagore*

◆ ◆ ◆

RIDDHI SANYAL

8.0   Learner Section 2 | Preliminary Practices Flute

Day 10, Day 11 – Play 2 notes at a time
Once gain stability on single notes, you can start playing 2 notes at a time. Please try to follow equal time signature for all notes.

Exercise 1: Play 2 same notes at a time
Simple example will illustrate how to practice this.

Convention	Time Sig	1	2	3	4	5	6	7	8
Indian	1	SS	RR	GG	mm	PP	DD	NN	ŜŜ
Western	1	CC	DD	EE	FF	GG	AA	BB	ĈĈ
Indian	2	ŜŜ	NN	DD	PP	mm	GG	RR	SS
Western	2	ĈĈ	BB	AA	GG	FF	EE	DD	CC

Exercise 1: Play 2 same notes at a time

Either of the notation conventions can be followed – Indian / Western.

This exercise can be played with a simple 4/4 Beat metronome.

For the initial days, you can keep the tempo very low as 60 – 80 (Beats Per Minute). All exercise notations are also created in **Sheet Music (Staff Notation)** for the better readability of the western followers. The initial exercises of the staff notation can be played in any instruments and it's not specific to Flute. Well you should not identically compare the exercises on Indian and Western as the beating patterns and the representations are different. Staff notation or sheet music has unique style to represent the beating pattern, measures, tempo, gaps and the repeats. The 4/4 measures in western can accommodate 16 quarter notes and ¾ will contain 12 quarter notes. You will gradually learn the staff notation system from the basics.

Coming back to the same exercise of playing two (2) notes at same time, in staff notation is shown with multiple ways. The starting 16 measures are shown with **Half (½) Notes**. Next 8 measures, from 17 – 24, the same notes are changed into **Quarter (1/4) notes**. Therefore, the playing tempo should be double while playing the measures from 17 – 24. Hence, you should start with very show tempo like 60 – 80 BPM. Then you should be able to play both sections of the staff notation 1. The staff notation / sheet music will help the learners to be comfortable on the notation conventions of Half note & Quarter notes.

RIDDHI SANYAL

Playing 2 Notes at a time

- For any Musical Instruments, by Riddhi Sanyal

Sheet Music 1: Play 2 Same Notes at a time

Exercise 2: Play 2 sequential notes at a time

During this exercise, we will practice two sequential notes on each time signature with a slower tempo as previous one (60 – 80 BPM).

RIDDHI SANYAL

Convention	Time Sig	1	2	3	4	5	6	7	8
Indian	1	SR	RG	Gm	mP	PD	DN	NŜ	R̂Ŝ
Western	1	CD	DE	EF	FG	GA	AB	BĈ	ĎĈ
Indian	2	ŜN	ND	DP	Pm	mG	GR	RS	N̲S̲
Western	2	ĈB	BA	AG	GF	FE	ED	DC	B̲C̲

Exercise 2: Play 2 sequential notes at a time

The equivalent sheet music shows the same in two rhythms. Similar to the previous Sheet Music practice, the same notes are created in Half (1/2) notes from 1-16 measures and on Quarter (1/4) notes from 17-24 measures. This will give confidence to the learner to play at either Half note speed or at quarter note speed. Another reason for two rhythms are to make the learner comfortable at both Half & Quarter notes.

Playing 2 Sequential Notes at a time

- For any Musical Instruments, by Riddhi Sanyal

RIDDHI SANYAL

Sheet Music 2: Play 2 Sequential Notes at a time

Day 12 – Play alternate notes

The alternate notes like SG, Rm, GP ... should be played and practiced. In this exercise, we will learn playing alternative notes at both upward & downward direction. Practicing more and more these exercises will orchestrate your fingers with your mind and thought. Initially these exercises should be played with lower tempo. However, down the line once you are familiar, you can increase the tempo until you are comfortable.

Convention	Time Sig	1	2	3	4	5	6	7	8
Indian	1	SG	Rm	GP	mD	PN	DŜ	NR̂	ŜŜ
Western	1	CE	DF	EG	FA	GB	AĈ	BĎ	ĈĈ
Indian	2	ŜD	NP	Dm	PG	mR	GS	RN	SS
Western	2	ĈA	BG	AF	GE	FD	EC	DB	CC

Exercise 3: Play alternate notes

Similarly, on the Sheet Music, the representation is given below. This exercise carries the same instruction to play like the previous ones.

RIDDHI SANYAL

Play Alternative Notes

- For any Musical Instruments, by Riddhi Sanyal

Sheet Music 3: Play Alternative Notes

RIDDHI SANYAL

Day 13, Day 14 – Learn to play with 8 Beat (4+4) Taal

Well, you have already started practicing with 8 beat with the earlier exercises. For a beginner in Indian Music, some commonly used Taal (also termed as Tal / Tala) are given below with the sample Bol[8] / stroke.

Name	Beats	Division	Bol / Strokes commonly used with Sam(+) & Khali (0)															
Tintal	16	4+4+4+4	Dha	Dhin	Dhin	Dha	Dha	Dhin	Dhin	Dha	Na [0]	Tin	Tin	Ta	Tete	Dhin	Dhin	ha
			+1	2	3	4	5	6	7	8	9	10	11	12	13	14	15	16
Ektal	12	3+3+3+3	Dhin	Dhin	Dha Ge	TiRa KiTa	Tu	Na	Ka [0]	Ta	Dha Ge	TiRa KiTa	Dhin	Na				
			+1	2	3	4	5	6	7	8	9	10	11	12				
Chau-tal	12	4+4+4 or 2+2+2+2+2+2	Dha	Dha	Den	Ta	Kat	TaGe	Den	Ta	TiRa	Kete	GaDi	Ghe Na				
			+1	2	3	4	5	6	7	8	9	10	11	12				
Jhap-tal	10	2+3+2+3	Dhin	Na	Dhin	Dhin	Na	Ti [0]	Na	Dhin	Dhin	Na						
			+1	2	3	4	5	6	7	8	9	10						
Keher wa	8	4+4 or 2+2+2+2	Dha	Ge	Na	Ti	Na [0]	Ge	Dhin	Na								
			+1	2	3	4	5	6	7	8								
Rupak	7	3+2+2	Tin	Tin	Na	Dhin	Na	Dhin	Na									
			+1	2	3	4	5	6	7									
Dadra	6	3+3	Dha	Dhin	Na	Na [0]	Tin	Na										
			+1	2	3	4	5	6										

Table 4: Indian Taal (Rhythms) with common Bol / Strokes

The symbol (+ or **x**) represents the first position and termed as *Som*. The entire *Bol* repeats from this *Som* position. Generally the middle of the *Bol* contains the sign (0) *Khali / Phak*. The heavy beating sound "Dha" is transformed into lighter sound "Ta" or "Na" from this 0th position.

The basic Taal with strokes are given for a beginner to identify the Taal and as we grow, our objective will be to play with the Taal. Our exercises will mainly use Keherwa (4+4), Dadra (3+3) and Tintal (4+4+4+4).

Coming back to our current exercise, following one is created on the consideration of playing single / double notes in same time signature or same beat. The exercise follows simple 4+4 beats / Keherwa Tal. The notes are designed for the beginner Flutist with most of the consecutive notes to play. Practice as many times (ex: 30 times) in a session.

---

[8] *Bol or Theka is the pattern of strokes of a Taal for playing in percussion instruments like Tabla, Mridangam, Sri Khol etc. It's equivalent to the pattern of beats in drum for a rhythm (4, 6, 8, 16 beats).*

RIDDHI SANYAL

Convention	Time Sig	1	2	3	4	5	6	7	8
Indian	1	S	R	Gm	P	D	P	mG	R
Western	1	C	D	EF	G	A	G	FE	D
Indian	2	N̲	S	RG	m	P	m	GR	S
Western	2	B	C	DE	F	G	F	ED	C
Indian	3	G	m	PD	N	D	P	mG	R
Western	3	E	F	GA	B	A	G	FE	D
Indian	4	Ŝ	N	DP	m	G	R	SN̲	S
Western	4	Ĉ	B	AG	F	E	D	CB̲	C

Exercise 4: Play Notes with 8 Beat Rhythm (Keherwa Tal)

The Sheet Music continues below. The tempo can be slower as 60 – 80 BPM.

Play Notes with 4/4 (8 Beats)

- For any Musical Instruments, by Riddhi Sanyal

Sheet Music 4: Play Notes with 4/4 beats

Day 15 – Learn Rest / Gap

Once you are comfortable playing with beats, you should know the off beats or Rests / Gaps or silence. In Indian notation, we have

- ✓ Whole rest / gap is denoted by symbol –
- ✓ Half Rest is denoted by : with notes (Ex ':S' means ½ rest then S)
- ✓ 1/3 Rest is denoted by : with notes (Ex 'S:S' means 1/3 rest between 2 S)
- ✓ ¼ Rest is denoted by : in notes (Ex: 'SSSS :G:G' shows ¼ rest G twice)

RIDDHI SANYAL

This exercise we will start with whole rest. For the sake to simplicity to follow, Indian and Western Notations are separately provided for each exercises. Learners can choose any one convention as they wish.

Convention	Time Sig	1	2	3	4	5	6	7	8
Indian	1	S	–	R	G	P	–	m	G
Indian	2	R	–	G	m	P	–	P	–
Indian	3	D	–	P	m	G	–	R	S
Indian	4	P	m	G	R	S	–	S	–

Exercise 5A: Play Notes with Whole Rests – Indian Notation

Convention	Time Sig	1	2	3	4	5	6	7	8
Western	1	C	–	D	E	G	–	F	E
Western	2	D	–	E	F	G	–	G	–
Western	3	A	–	G	F	E	–	D	C
Western	4	G	F	E	D	C	–	C	–

Exercise 5B: Play Notes with Whole Rests – Western Notation

The Sheet Music has more details than the Indian convention. As mentioned earlier, you cannot identically compare the Notations of Gaps with Indian & Staff notations, as the representation is different.

This Sheet Music has additional details to display Whole Gaps and then Half, Quarter and Eighth Gaps. It has the equivalent Whole, Half, Quarter and Eighth Notes.

You may start with 120 BPM or slower at per the comfort level.

RIDDHI SANYAL

Learn Rest / Gap

- For any Musical Instruments, by Riddhi Sanyal

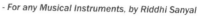

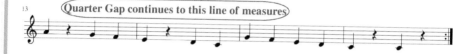

Sheet Music 5: Learn Rest / Gap for Whole, Half, Quarter and Eighth Gaps

Day 16 – Learn ½ Notes and ½ Rests

We will learn to play the half notes along with half rests in the 8 beat Keherwa Tal. In this exercise, ½ rests are used in front of notes (:Ŝ or :P) as well as after the notes (S:). Prior to this exercise, we have already gone through the scenario of ½ Notes on exercise 1, 2, 3 and 4. We have observed the 2 notes are used in same time signature. Similarly, in this exercise also we have used ½ notes (GG, PD etc).

RIDDHI SANYAL

Convention	Time Sig	1	2	3	4	5	6	7	8
Indian	1	GG	m	PD	:Ŝ	R̂Ŝ	ND	P	−
Indian	2	Gm	:P	DP	:m	Pm	GR	S:	S:

Exercise 6: Play ½ Notes with 1/2 Rests − Indian Notation

Continuing on the staff notation, it has little different structure. To get symmetry,
Indian 1 Note / Rest / Time Signature == Quarter (1/4) Note / Rest in staff
Indian ½ Note / Rest == Eighth (1/8) Note / Rest in staff

Play Eighth(1/8) Note and 1/8 Rests

- For any Musical Instruments, Notation is touching the area needed for Flute Practice. by Riddhi Sanyal

Sheet Music 6: Play Eighth Notes and Rests

Day 17, 18, 19 − Recap with more Exercises

During our first phase of learning, we have learnt the basics of playing flute. Summarizing the key intakes −

- ❖ Learnt how to hold the flute & produce stable sound.
- ❖ Now we know to play the entire notes **SRGmPDNŜ** in both directions.
- ❖ We are trying hard to make a consistent sound on every note.
- ❖ We know the whole note, ½ notes.
- ❖ Now we are comfortable on simple 8 beat rhythm.
- ❖ We have learned the Gaps, ½ Gaps that helps to pause for certain intervals during the music.
- ❖ We have started playing 2 notes at a moment (single beat).
- ❖ Learnt the Indian Notation system and sheet music system.

During the initial stage of playing, everyone needs to pay attention more on some combinations. Such as −

- ➤ m P | P m
- ➤ G m P | D P m
- ➤ N Ŝ R̂ | Ĝ R̂ Ŝ

RIDDHI SANYAL

- ➢ P D̲ N̲ | S N̲ D̲
- ➢ G P m D | P m G R
- ➢ S G m P | D m G R
- ➢ S R S G | m P D N | Ŝ D P m | G R S N̲

Exercise 7: Learn 6 Beat – Indian Convention

These combinations may be practiced more and more (say 30 times) every day to gain stability and confidence on the flute.

The Sheet Music continues on certain weak areas which need more practice. It follows the same notes in a 4/4 beat structure.

Customized Exercises For Flute Practice

- by Riddhi Sanyal

Sheet Music 7: Customized exercise for Flute practice

RIDDHI SANYAL

Day 20 – Progression on 3 notes at a time

Playing three notes at a time is very common in Indian & Western music. It's generally given in the initial stage of vocal / all instrumental practices. While playing in Flute, learner should always try to play in same tempo / rhythm. Higher octave notes and lower octave notes are also included in the practice. That will enrich the player to play beyond the octave. Set a lower tempo to start with (60). Once comfortable, you may increase the tempo without breaking. Take 3 notes in a time signature in 1 breath. Then gradually increase it, like 3-4 time signatures in 1 breath.

Time Sig	1	2	3	4	5	6	7	8
1	SRG	RGm	GmP	mPD	PDN	DNŜ	NŜR̂	ŜR̂Ĝ
2	ŜND	NDP	DPm	PmG	mGR	GRS	RSN	SND

Exercise 8: Play 3 notes at a time – Indian Convention

Sheet Music is created with ¾ Tempo (3 beats in 1 measure). For better readability, 8 measures are given in 1 line in this case. The notes are touching the Higher & Lower octave notes as well to give you complete practice with a rhythm.

Play Progression on 3 Notes in 6 Beats

- For any Musical Instruments, Notation is touching the area needed for Flute Practice. by Riddhi Sanyal

Sheet Music 8: Play Progression on 3 Notes in 6 beats (3/4)

RIDDHI SANYAL

Day 21 – Progression on 4 notes at a time

Playing 4 notes together is also very common in Indian & Western music. We have included lower and higher octave notes to improve learner's efficiency. Same guidelines follow here like – slower tempo, play one time signature in one breath and gradually increase.

Time Sig	1	2	3	4	5	6	7	8
1	P̱ḎṈS	ḎṈSR	ṈSRG	SRGm	RGmP	GmPD	mPDN	PDNŜ
2	ṁĜR̂Ŝ	ĜR̂ŜN	R̂ŜND	ŜNDP	NDPm	DPmG	PmGR	mGRS

Exercise 9: Play 4 notes at a time – Indian Convention

Sheet Music shows the beating pattern (4/4). You can take your own tempo and try to increase with more practice.

Play Progression on 4 Notes in 8 Beats

- For any Musical Instruments, Notation is touching the area needed for Flute Practice. by Riddhi Sanyal

Sheet Music 9: Play Progression on 4 Notes in 8 beats (4/4)

RIDDHI SANYAL

Day 23 – Learn to play with 6 Beat (3+3) Taal – Dadra

Considering beginner player, composition is created with simple 3 + 3 beat Dadra Taal. The complete notation can be played 5-6 times to get a feel for that. You may practice this piece 30 – 40 times in 1 session to be formalized with the Taal. The Tempo can be set 60 – 80 BPM.

Time Sig	1	2	3	4	5	6
1	P	D	P	R	G	m
2	N	D	P	G	R	S
3	D̲	S	R	m	–	m
4	N̲	R	G	P	–	P
5	DN	D	P	mp	m	R
6	Ŝ	N	D	P	m	G
7	N	D	P	m	P	m
8	Gm	P	m	G	R	S

Exercise 10: Learn 6 Beat – Indian Convention

The equivalent Sheet Music is almost similar to Indian in this case.

Play Notes in 6 Beats

- For Flute Practice. by Riddhi Sanyal

Sheet Music 10: Play Notes on 6 beats (3/4) in Dadra Taal

Day 24, Day 25 – Revision & Practice lessons with Sargam

Practice is the only way to gain more control of every notes. For that, its recommended to play every tune for 30 – 40 times initially. After playing few times, you can play the exercises by closing your eyes. Then only you can play from your heart and not from the notation.

So far we have learnt to play alternate notes, progressions, rest notes, ½ rests and ½ notes, 3 notes a time, 4 notes a time, lower octave notes, higher octave notes, 8 beat Taal (Keherwa) and 6 beat Taal (Dadra). When you practice the next exercise, it does not mean that you are not doing it for earlier. It is always recommended to revise the earlier exercises frequently. More you play; you will note the difference in your playing on the same exercise.

RIDDHI SANYAL

Time Sig	1	2	3	4	5	6	7	8
1	S	–	S	R	G	m	P	D
2	R	–	R	G	m	P	D	N
3	G	–	G	m	P	D	N	Ŝ
4	R̂	Ŝ	D	m	P	G	R	S
5	N̲	S	–	G	m	Pm	G	–
6	R	G	–	m	P	DP	m	–
7	G	m	–	P	D	NŜ	R̂	–
8	Ŝ	–	N	–	DP	mG	R	S

Exercise 11: Revision & Additional Exercise – Indian Convention

The Sheet Music follows identical structure for this one.

RIDDHI SANYAL

Revision Exercise for Flute on 8 Beats

- For Flute Practice. by Riddhi Sanyal

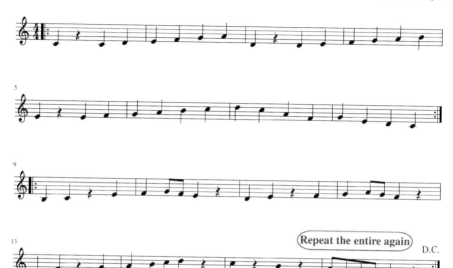

Sheet Music 11: Revision exercise for Flute on 8 beat

"Many great works of art, poetry, and music are inspired by astral memories. The desire to do noble, beautiful things here on Earth is also often a carryover of astral experiences between a person's earth lives." - Paramahansa Yogananda

RIDDHI SANYAL

9.0 Learner Section 3 | Play Music & Songs in Flute

Day 26 – Play Simple tune – Happy Birthday

It's universal to start with Happy Birthday tune. We will start the tune from S (C). Here we will learn a new note – Komal / Flat ni (Bb). Hence to proceed, we will first learn the note and then the HBD tune.

Playing Komal (Flat) ni, Notation Symbol = n, Western: Bb w.r.t. C Scale

To play Komal ni, 1st to 4th holes should be blocked completely, 5th hole partially & 6th Hole open.

- ✓ Place the Left Hand Index finger to block the **first** hole completely.
- ✓ Keep Left hand middle finger to block the **second** hole completely.
- ✓ Use the Left hand Ring finger to block **third** hole completely.
- ✓ Keep the Right Hand index finger to block **fourth** Hole completely.
- ✓ No leakage of air is important on these four holes.
- ✓ Right hand middle finger should block the **fifth** hole partially around 50% (for someone it may be blocked till 75%). Depending on the blowing pressure, flutist need to control the amount to block.
- ✓ Blowing pressure is **higher** than normal.
- ✓ One able to play the note n, practice n D P, P D n, P D n Ŝ, Ŝ n D P, …

Figure 16: Flute position - ni - Notation symbol n. (Bb w.r.t. C Scale)

Coming back to the HBD exercise, we will follow 6 beats. You will apply your learning to play the komal ni – n (Bb) by this exercise.

Time Sig	1	2	3	4	5	6
1	SS	R	S	m	G	–
2	SS	R	S	P	m	–
3	SS	Ŝ	D	m	G	R
4	nn	D	m	P	m	–

Exercise 12: Play Happy Birthday – Indian Convention

RIDDHI SANYAL

Please note HBD can also be played starting from the lower octave Pa – P̲ without any flat notes. You can try out yourself.

Those who are following western notation, for them the western notation is created for Happy Birthday Tune. For simplicity its 6 beats (3/4). The scale is always in C for western Sheet Music.

Sheet Music 12: Play Happy Birthday

Please note that Happy Birthday can be played in 4/4 beats also. You can try that yourself.

Day 27 – Play Simple tune – 'Twinkle Twinkle'
Starting with the simple tune so that any learner can play them by heart. Please play at your comfortable tempo.

Time Sig	1	2	3	4	5	6	7	8
1	S	S	P	P	D	D	P	–
2	m	m	G	G	R	R	S	–
3	P	–	Pm	m	G	G	R	–
4	P	–	Pm	m	G	G	R	–

Exercise 13: Play 'Twinkle Twinkle' – Indian Convention

Learn "Twinkle Twinkle" in Sheet Music from the below sheet music. It's in standard 4/4 beats. To repeat the first line, D.C al Fine and Segno symbol is used.

RIDDHI SANYAL

Twinkle Twinkle

- Simplified for Flute, by Riddhi Sanyal

Sheet Music 13: Play 'Twinkle Twinkle'

Day 28 – Play 'We Shall Overcome'

To play with confidence, another known tune is given for practice – We Shall Overcome. This song is there almost with every language. You can play this from your heart. Notation is given as reference.

Time Sig	1	2	3	4	5	6	7	8
1	P	P	D	D	P	:m	G	–
2	P	P	D	D	P	:m	G	Gm
3	P	P	D	N	Ŝ	–	R̂	:Ŝ
4	N	–	DN	:D	P	–	D	N
5	Ŝ	Ŝ	N	D	P	–	–	–
6	D	D	P	m	G	–	–	Gm
7	P	P	S	m	G	–	R	–
8	S	–	–	–	–	–	–	Gm

Exercise 14: Play 'We Shall Overcome' – Indian Convention

RIDDHI SANYAL

Practice for 40 times and play at least 2-3 times during performance. During repeat, you should play the last note (8, 8 time signature) – 'Gm', but at the end / last cycle, you should not play the last note 'Gm'. It is only kept for repeating the entire song.

Enjoy the song in Sheet Music. 4/4 beats are used as the song demands. The entire song is repeated using repeat symbol.

We Shall Overcome

- Simplified for Flute, by Riddhi Sanyal

Sheet Music 14: Play 'We Shall Overcome'

Day 29 – Play 'Jamaican Farewell'

Another famous musical tune that can be played in any instrument and in flute too. Idea behind providing the simple and cool music is to play them spontaneously from insight. Anyone can co-relate these in the choice of his instrument. We will learn to play Jamaican Farewell in little bit faster tempo (120 - 140) as the tune demands. Here is the notation for all.

Time Sig	1	2	3	4	5	6	7	8
1	: P	: P	P	P	DN	: Ŝ	–	ND
2	P :	P	m :	m	GG	mP	–	–
3	: P	: P	P	P	DN	: Ŝ	–	ND
4	P :	P	m :	m	GG	RS	–	GP
5	S :	S	G :	G	RR	: m	–	GR
6	N̲	N̲	R	R	SR	: G	–	–
7	: S	SS	G	G	R	R	m	m
8	G	G	R	R	GR	: S	–	–

Exercise 15: Play 'Jamaican Farewell' – Indian Convention

Notation is given for single time. It should be played at least 2–3 times while performing. But for practice, initially you should play 20 – 30 times.

Sheet Music is created on the same 4/4 beat in C Scale. Playing this type of song will help to understand the beats in much better way as there are lot of ½ notes and ½ gaps.

RIDDHI SANYAL

Jamaican Farewell

- Simplified for Flute, by Riddhi Sanyal

Sheet Music 15: Play Jamaican Farewell

Day 30 – Play 'Do A Deer' from Sound of Music

We should never forget to play Do-A-Deer as it depicts the basics touching all the notes. That's why beginners are always recommended to play this one in any instrument. Please note that there is a Tempo change in between. The 2nd section becomes faster than the first section. The column 'Times To Play' denotes the number of times to play that section surrounded by brackets (...). The column 'Return to TimeSig' will denote where to return after that section is played for denoted number of times (here it's 2 times). It's recommended to conclude the song by playing the section 1 again. So you can return from line 14 to line 1 while 2nd time playing that section.

RIDDHI SANYAL

Time Sig	1	2	3	4	5	6	7	8	Times to play	Tempo	Return to Sig
1	(S	:R	GG	:S	G	S	GG	-			
2	R	:G	mm	GR	m	-	-	-			
3	G	:m	P	:G	P	G	P	-			
4	m	:P	DD	Pm	D	-	-	-	2	120	After 2 times go to 9
5	P	:S	RG	mP	D	-	-	-			
6	D	:R	Gm	PD	N	-	-	-			
7	N	:G	mP	DN	Ŝ	-	-	ŜN			
8	D	m	N	P	Ŝ	:P	G	R)			
9	(S	G	G	-	G	P	P	-	2		11
10	R	m	m	-	D	N	N	-)			
11	(P	-	S	-	D	-	m	-		160	
12	G	-	S	-	R	-	-	-	2		1
13	P	-	S	-	D	-	N	-			
14	Ŝ	-	R̂	-	Ŝ	-	-	-)			

Exercise 16: Play 'DO A DEER' – Indian Convention

Try the Sheet Music too. This type of song will help you to learn staff notation quite easily. Well this is created in 4/4 beats. The time signature and repeats may not be look identical in staff notations on compared to Indian convention. Primary reason is that 8 beats are shown at in a row for Indian convention whereas mostly 16 beats are kept in Sheet Music in a row / frame as that's standard for Sheet Music.

RIDDHI SANYAL

Do A Deer, A Female Deer

- Simplified for Flute, by Riddhi Sanyal

Sheet Music 16: Play 'Do A Deer a Female Deer'

RIDDHI SANYAL

Day 31 – Play Scottish tune 'Auld Lang Syne'

Until now, we played those musical pieces that are recommended for any new musicians in any instrument. However, this Scottish tune, 'Auld Lang Syne' suites bowing instruments like woodwinds / violin. Learner will now be able to differentiate this one from the others while playing in Flute.

Time Sig	1	2	3	4	5	6	7	8
1	–	–	–	–	–	–	–	P̲
2	S	: S	S	G	R	: S	R :	GR
3	S	: S	G	P	D	–	–	D
4	P	: G	G	S	R	: S	R :	GR
5	S	: D̲	D̲	P̲	S	–	–	P̲
6	S	: S	S	G	R	: S	R :	GR
7	S	: S	G	P	D	–	–	D
8	P	: G	G	S	R	: S	R :	GR
9	S	: D̲	D̲	P̲	S	–	–	D
10	P	: G	G	S	R	: S	R :	D
11	P	: G	G	P	D	–	–	Ŝ
12	D	: P	P	S	R	: S	R :	GR
13	S	: D̲	D̲	P̲	S	–	–	D
14	P	: G	G	S	R	: S	R :	D
15	P	: G	G	P	D	–	–	Ŝ
16	D	: P	P	S	R	: S	R :	GR
17	S	: D̲	D̲	P̲	S	–	–	–

Exercise 17: Play 'Auld Lang Syne' – Indian Convention

RIDDHI SANYAL

The notation starts from lower octave P̱. Time Signature 2-5 and 6-9 are almost identical except the last note. It's shown in different color for better readability. Similarly line 10-13 and 14-17 are identical except the last note. We will practice on slower rhythm (Ex: Tempo 100 - 120) to match with original tune.

This melodious tune is so catchy that World's Greatest Poet, *Gurudeb Sri Rabindranath Tagore* had composed famous *Rabindra Sangeet 'Purano Sei Diner Kotha'* based on this tone.

The Sheet Music of 'Auld Lang Syne' is created in 4/4 in C Scale.

Auld Lang Syne

- Simplified for Flute, by Riddhi Sanyal

Sheet Music 17: Play 'Auld Lang Syne'

RIDDHI SANYAL

Day 32 – Play simple Hindi Song – A Chal Ke Tujhe

This one is again selected as one of the nice and simple tune in any instrument and more soothing in flute. This famous Hindi song was sang by legendary singer *Kishore Kumar* and it's his own music composition. You have to play <u>Tibra Ma (symbol M)</u> in one of the note in this song. That is present at last note of the Time Signature 9. Taal of this song is Keherwa (8 beat), but *Tabla* / Percussion bol played 2 tones together (DhaGe NaTi NaGe DhiNa). For example, 1 Music Note contains 2 Taal strokes. Hence for a western musician it will look like 4 beats are played.

For better reading, the notation is shown in different colors for *Sthayi* (Initial section) and Antara of the song.

Time Sig	1	2	3	4	5	6	7	8	Times to play	Return to Time Sig
①	–	–	–	–	–	–	–	P̲		
②	(S	SR	S	P̲	S	SR	S	P̲		
③	S	SR	G	mG	mG	R	–	P̲	2	
④	R	RG	R	P̲	R	RG	R	SR		
⑤	N̲	N̲S	P	Pm	G	–	–	P̲		
⑥	S	SR	G	mG	S	–	–	)	(G	② – 1
⑦	(S	SR	GP	PD	P	G	–	Gm	2	
⑧	P	PP	D	Pm	D	P	–	)	(	⑦ – 1
⑨	D	DP	DP	mG	m	R	–	MM	1	
⑩	P	Pm	GR	mG	R	S	–	P̲		② – 1

Exercise 18: Play 'A Chal Ke Tujhe' – Indian Convention

Repeats are explained in the "Times to Play" column and where to return is shown in last column. Brackets are used to denote additionally to which note to be played in 1st & 2nd time; Ex: for the first time P̲ will be played in the ⑥ -8 position, but during repeat GP will be played in that position. Similarly at ⑧ - 8, first time GP and 2nd time PD will be played.

Staff notations are given in 4/4 beats. Playing this peaceful song tune will make you comfortable all around the Flute.

RIDDHI SANYAL

A Chal Ke Tujhe

Composed and Sang by Kishore Kumar

- Simplified for Flute, by Riddhi Sanyal

Fine

D.S. al Fine

Sheet Music 18: Play Hindi song tune 'A Chal Ke Tujhe'

RIDDHI SANYAL

Day 33 – Play simple Rabindra Sangeet – Phule Phule

'*Phule Phule*', Tune of flowers, is one of the most melodious *Rabindra Sangeet*. This song is chosen as it suites flute more than others. Learning this, a beginner will get the flavor of *Rabindra Sangeet*, a new genre of music in the history of Indian music. Gurudeb Sri Rabindranath Tagore has composed around 2500 songs, which are still famous and maintained its originality after 100 or more years. Depth with words and music in *Rabindra Sangeet* will take you in different dimensions. We will play 'Phule Phule' in lower pace (around 120 tempo) in 6 beat rhythm (Dadra Taal).

Time Sig	1	2	3	4	5	6	Times to play	Return to Time Sig
①	m	–	m	P	m	P		
②	D	Ŝ	D	P	m	P	2	
③	D	P	m	m	R	S		
④	S	R	m	m	–	–		① - 1
⑤	S	–	S	SR	m:	m		
⑥	m	P	P	P	D	P	2	
⑦	m	–	G	m	D	P		
⑧	m	G	m	R	S	–		⑤ - 1
⑨	Ŝ	–	ŜR̂	Ŝ	n	D	2	
⑩	n	–	nŜ	n	D	P		⑨ - 1
⑪	Ŝ	D	m	Ŝ	D	m	1	
⑫	Ŝ	n	D	P	–	–		
⑬	S	m	m	P	m	P		
⑭	D	Ŝ	D	P	m	P	1	
⑮	D	P	m	m	R	S		
⑯	S	R	m	m	–	–		① - 1

Exercise 19: Play 'Phule Phule – Flowers – Rabindra Sangeet' – Indian Convention

RIDDHI SANYAL

Sheet Music is created for Phule Phule. The song is in ¾ beats. This song is illustrated in details through this sheet music video.

Phule Phule

A Rabindranath Tagore Song *Simplified for Flute, by Riddhi Sanyal*

Sheet Music 19: Play 'Phule Phule'

RIDDHI SANYAL

Day 34 – Play Hindi Bhajan – Om Jai Jagadish Hare

Flutes are appropriate choice of instruments to Indian *Bhajans* or Prayers. One of the most famous Bhajan is illustrated here. Jagadish is another name of Sri Krishna. This bhajan is dedicated to Jagadish or Sri Krishna. Keherwa (8 Beat) can be played in a different flavor to match Bhajan.

Song Sec	Time Sig	1	2	3	4	5	6	7	8	Times to play	Return to Sig
Sthayi	①	S	–	S	S	S	RS	N	S		
	②	R	–	–	–	–	–	R	G		
	③	m	–	P	P	D	P	m	G		
	④	mG	R	–	–	–	–	–	–		
	⑤	R	G	R	G	m	–	m	G		
	⑥	R	G	S	–	R	G	R	G	2	
	⑦	m	–	m	G	R	G	S	–		
	⑧	S	S	R	R	G	R	S	N		
	⑨	D	–	–	–	–	–	R	R		
	⑩	R	–	R	R	G	R	S	N		
	⑪	S	–	–	–	–	–	–	–		① - 1
Antara	⑫	R	–	S	N	R	–	S	N		
	⑬	R	–	S	N	R	–	S	–		
	⑭	P	–	m	–	G	–	R	S		
	⑮	R	–	–	–	–	–	P	P		
	⑯	P	–	m	–	G	–	R	S		
	⑰	R	–	–	–	–	–	–	–		
	⑱	R	G	R	G	m	–	m	G	1	
	⑲	R	G	S	–	R	G	R	G		
	⑳	m	–	m	G	R	G	S	–		
	21	S	S	R	R	G	R	S	N		
	22	D	–	–	–	–	–	R	R		
	23	R	–	R	R	G	R	S	N		
	24	S	–	–	–	–	–	–	–		① - 1

Exercise 20: Play 'Om Jai Jagadish Hare' – Indian Convention

This notation is created considering for the beginner players. Actual notation will include more notes in some area.

Om Jai Jagadish Hare

Sri Krishna Bhajan, this nice tune is also used for Mata Ganga Arati at Varanasi & Hardwar

- Simplified for Flute, by Riddhi Sanyal

RIDDHI SANYAL

Sheet Music 20: Play 'Om Jai Jagadish Hare'

Day 35, Day 36, Day 37 – Revision & Further Lessons

During this 2nd Phase of learning (Day 20 – Day 37), we have improved our skills and learnt music from all around the world. The exercises are created and organized in such a way that a newcomer can overcome the hurdle one by one after following them. Summarizing the learning in this section –

- We have learnt to follow the rhythm.
- Gained knowledge in 6 beats and 8 beats rhythm.
- Learnt to play simple tunes like Happy Birthday, Twinkle Twinkle and gradually reach a position to play long tunes / songs.
- We have learned to repeat a section of musical piece.
- Gained knowledge on minor (flat / sharp) notes like in HBD, we have learnt the Komal ni – symbolled is **n** (Bb w.r.t. C). Similarly learnt the Tibra Ma – symbolled as **M** (F# w.r.t. C).
- Observed how a *Bhajan* can be played in Flute.
- Learn to play 3 notes in a beats and similarly 4 notes in a beat.
- Most important is that we have gained stability on every note and we can stay at each note for 3-5 seconds.

This will conclude this 3rd section of the learning contents. To conclude this, let us play an 8 beat ceremony music which we generally play during end of a function / show. This is composed by Guruji Sri D. Madhusudan. Hope you all will enjoy this –

RIDDHI SANYAL

Time Sig	1	2	3	4	5	6	7	8
1	SS	SS	S	G	R	–	S	P̲
2	SS	SS	S	G	R	–	–	–
3	SS	SS	S	G	R	–	S	P̲
4	SS	SS	S	G	R	–	G	m
5	PP	PP	P	D	P	–	R	–
6	mm	mm	m	D	P	–	–	–
7	PP	PP	P	D	P	–	R	–
8	mm	mm	m	D	P	–	D	N
9	ŜŜ	ŜŜ	Ŝ	P	NN	NN	N	m
10	DD	DD	P	R	S	–	D	N
11	ŜŜ	ŜŜ	Ŝ	P	NN	NN	N	m
12	DD	DD	P	R	S	–	–	–
13	GG	GG	G	G	RR	RR	R	R
14	mm	mm	G	m	G	–	–	–
15	GG	GG	G	G	RR	RR	R	R
16	mm	mm	G	m	G	–	Ŝ	R̂
17	ŜŜ	ŜŜ	Ŝ	P	NN	NN	N	m
18	DD	DD	P	R	S	–	D	N
19	ŜŜ	ŜŜ	Ŝ	P	NN	NN	N	m
20	DD	DD	P	R	S	–	–	–

Exercise 21: Play 'Closing Ceremony Harmony Music'

Sheet Music is created for this song. It's in 4/4 beat.

RIDDHI SANYAL

Closing Ceremony Song

Composed by Sri D. Madhusudan

- Converted to staff notation, by Riddhi Sanyal

Sheet Music 21: 'Closing Ceremony Harmony Music'

Until this point, we have learnt different flavors of music from various portion of our planet. From now onwards, we will primarily learn Indian Classical Ragas in Flute in the next section of the book.

RIDDHI SANYAL

10.0   Learner Section 4 | Play Indian Classical Ragas

Day 38 to Day 42 – Raga Hansadhwani

Until now, we have played known music to gain confidence. From now onwards for the rest of the book, we will mainly concentrate on the Ragas (also termed as *Raag / Ragam*). Before we start, first question comes, what is **Raga**? There may be several answers. To my realization, one **Raga** depicts the state of mind on that time of the day within the current environment. Some of the Ragas lead to Peace, Soft melodious, Calm whereas some are Agile in nature.

We will start with Raga Hansadhwani (also termed as *Hamsadhvani*). Raga Hansadhwani was originally developed in Carnatic music and brought into Hindustani Classical. I remember my Gurudeb to provide me this Raga first. There are several reasons like

- ✓ It contains only 5 notes out of 7
- ✓ All are major notes, no flat / sharp
- ✓ Both side (to play upward / downward direction) are open to play
- ✓ This Raga is suitable to play in Flute more than string instruments

We will follow certain structure to learn a Raga. After the first one, you will understand it better.

Direction of Play:

Upward - *Arohana*					
Indian	S	R	G	P	N	Ŝ
Western	C	D	E	G	B	C'

Table 5: Raga Hansadhwani – Upward direction / Arohana

Downward - *Avarohana*					
Indian	Ŝ	N	P	G	R	S
Western	C'	B	G	E	D	C

Table 6: Raga Hansadhwani – Downward direction / Avarohana

Timings of Raga[9]: Second quarter of night.

---

[9] *Timings of Raga - It is recommend practicing any time a day. However, when you are playing for 1-2 hours at a single stretch, or perform in a function, it's always recommended to follow the timings of Raga.*

RIDDHI SANYAL

Thaat: Bilaval
Vadi | **Primary Note**: R (Re / D w.r.t. C)
Samavadi | **Secondary Note**: P (Pa / G w.r.t. C)

Chalan | *Pakad* | **Progression of Notes**:

Alaap: The initial mood of the raga comes with the gentle and smooth playing of the notes and that is the **Alaap** of Raga. There should not be any beats for this initial Alaap[10]. More time pause is denoted as "...", short time pause is denoted by single dot ".". Alaap can be different for every time you play the flute and obviously from person to person. The mood of the Raga needs to be present during the Alaap.

S ... N̲ S ... N̲ P ... P N̲ . N̲ S ...
S R ... N̲ S R ... N̲ P . N̲ S R ... G R S...
S R G ... N̲ S R ... P N̲ S ...
N̲ S R G ... R G P ... R G P . R G ...
G R . G P ... P N P ... R G . R P ...
G P N ... N Ŝ ... Ŝ ... Ŝ R̂ . Ĝ R̂ ... Ŝ
Ŝ N P ... G P . N P ... P G P R ... R G S ...

Exercise 22: Raga Hansadhwani - Alaap

Bandish / Gat[11] (*Gata*) with few *Taan* to practice in Teentaal:

---

[10] *Advanced students or learners may practice the Jor in Alaap or play with a Taal such as Vilamvit Ektal. That discussion may be continued in future books for advanced level.*

[11] *Bandish or Gat (Gata) is the first two lines of the Raga with the Taal. The next section or verse is called Antara. That is typically line number 3 & 4. These four lines can be played as-is during the initial days of practice.*

RIDDHI SANYAL

Tabla Bol >>	(0) Na	Tin	Tin	Ta	TeTe	Dhin	Dhin	Dha	(+) Dha	Dhin	Dhin	Dha	Dha	Dhin	Dhin	Dha

Raga Section	Time Sig	1	2	3	4	5	6	7	8	9	10	11	12	13	14	15	16	Times to play	Return to sig
Gat	①	G	-	G	R	S	-	Ṇ	P	R	-	G	P	G	R	S	-	2	
Gat	②	Ṇ	P̲	Ṇ	S	R	-	P	R	G	P	-	R	G	R	S	-	2	① - 1
Antara	③	P	G	-	R	G	P	N	-	Ŝ	-	Ŝ	-	Ĝ	R̂	Ŝ	-	2	
Antara	④	N	-	P	-	P	N	P	R	G	P	G	R	G	R	S	-	2	① - 1
Taan 1	⑤									SR	GP	NŜ	NP	RG	PR	GR	S	1	
Tihai 1	⑥	(SR	GP	R)	(SR	GP	R)	(SR	GP									1	① - 9
Taan 2	⑦	ṆS	RG	PN	ŜR̂	ŜN	PR	GR	S	(SR	GP	NP	GS	R	-)	(SR	GP	1	
Tihai 2	⑧	NP	GS	R	-)	(SR	GP	NP	GS									1	① - 9
Taan 3	⑨	GP	RG	PN	PR	GR	SṆ	PṆ	SR	GP	NP	RG	PN	ŜN	PR	GR	S	2	① - 1
Taan 4	⑩	RG	RS	RG	PR	SR	GP	Ŝ	NP	RG	PN	R̂	ŜN	GR	GP	N	PG	1	
Taan 4	⑪	RS	GR	PG	NP	NŜ	NP	GR	S	(RG	PS	RG	PG	R	-)	(RG	PS	1	
Taan 4	⑫	RG	PG	R	-)	(RG	PS	RG	PG									1	① - 9
Taan 5	⑬	PR	GP	NP	G	SR	GP	NŜ	R̂	RG	RS	GP	GR	G	GR	G	GR	1	① - 1

Exercise 23: Raga Hansadwani (Shorter notation) – Indian Convention

Whenever you return to Bandish, play the Bandish for at least 2 times. The left column contains the labels of the Raga Section like Bandish / Gat, Antara, Taan[12]. Next to that is the Time Signature that is given straight forward without counting the repeated Gat & others. Teental contains 16 beats. 1st and 9th beats are very important. 1st beat contains *Khali* (shown as 0) and 9th beat is the *Sam* (also termed / pronounced as *Som* symbol, shown as +). Rightmost column shows "Return to TimeSig". There we can see that you have to return to mainly either at Khali / Sam – 1st or 9th position of the 1st line of the Gat. Prior to that rightmost column, we have "Times to Play". Considering the repeats and returning positions, this Raga is illustrated with entire notation in the next page. Same color convention is maintained for anyone to co-relate the shorter notation and the entire one. At the end, you can play the Gat for 3 times to conclude the Raga with final Tihai[13].

As this is the first Raga, **elaborated notation** has been created to detail out each of the repetitions, returning to Gat, then the Taan and so on. Comparing the shorter one

[12] *Taan is the area of Raga to generate the mood (Bhava) of the Raga. You can play any number of Taan till the mood is sustained. As the beat of the Taal is 16, Taan can be played in beats of 8, 16, 24, 32 and so on.*

[13] *Tihai – When same notes are repeated 3 times, it's called Tihai. This beautifies the representation of the Raga when it matches to the Som (+) or Phak (o) position of the Taal.*

RIDDHI SANYAL

and the elaborated one, you will get more clarity on the starting positon and returning position of each sections.

RIDDHI SANYAL

Tabla Bol >>	(0) Na	Tin	Tin	Ta	TeTe	Dhin	Dhin	Dha	(+) Dha	Dhin	Dhin	Dha	Dha	Dhin	Dhin	Dha
Raga Section / Time Sig	1	2	3	4	5	6	7	8	9	10	11	12	13	14	15	16
①	G	-	G	R	S	-	N̲	P̲	R	-	G	P	G	R	S	-
2	G	-	G	R	S	-	N̲	P̲	R	-	G	P	G	R	S	-
Bandish 3	N̲	P̲	N̲	S	R	-	P	R	G	P	-	R	G	R	S	-
4	N̲	P̲	N̲	S	R	-	P	R	G	P	-	R	G	R	S	-
5	G	-	G	R	S	-	N̲	P̲	R	-	G	P	G	R	S	-
6	G	-	G	R	S	-	N̲	P̲	R	-	G	P	G	R	S	-
Antara 7	P	G	-	R	G	P	N	-	Ŝ	-	Ŝ	-	Ĝ	R̂	Ŝ	-
8	P	G	-	R	G	P	N	-	Ŝ	-	Ŝ	-	Ĝ	R̂	Ŝ	-
9	N	-	P	-	P	N	P	R	G	P	G	R	G	R	S	-
10	N	-	P	-	P	N	P	R	G	P	G	R	G	R	S	-
11	G	-	G	R	S	-	N̲	P̲	R	-	G	P	G	R	S	-
12	G	-	G	R	S	-	N̲	P̲	R	-	G	P	G	R	S	-
Taan 1 13	G	-	G	R	S	-	N̲	P̲	SR	GP	NŜ	NP	RG	PR	GR	S
Tihai 1 14	(SR	GP	R)	(SR	GP	R)	(SR	GP	R	-	G	P	G	R	S	-
15	G	-	G	R	S	-	N̲	P̲	R	-	G	P	G	R	S	-
16	G	-	G	R	S	-	N̲	P̲	R	-	G	P	G	R	S	-
Taan 2 17	N̲S	RG	PN	ŜR̂	ŜN	PR	GR	S	(SR	GP	NP	GS	R	-)	(SR	GP
Tihai 2 18	NP	GS	R	-)	(SR	GP	NP	GS	R	-	G	P	G	R	S	-
19	G	-	G	R	S	-	N̲	P̲	R	-	G	P	G	R	S	-
20	G	-	G	R	S	-	N̲	P̲	R	-	G	P	G	R	S	-
Taan 3 21	GP	RG	PN	PR	GR	SN̲	P̲N̲	SR	GP	NP	RG	PN	ŜN	PR	GR	S
22	GP	RG	PN	PR	GR	SN̲	P̲N̲	SR	GP	NP	RG	PN	ŜN	PR	GR	S
23	G	-	G	R	S	-	N̲	P̲	R	-	G	P	G	R	S	-
24	G	-	G	R	S	-	N̲	P̲	R	-	G	P	G	R	S	-
Taan 4 25	RG	RS	RG	PR	SR	GP	Ŝ	NP	RG	PN	R̂	ŜN	GR	GP	N	PG
26	RS	GR	PG	NP	NŜ	NP	GR	S	(RG	PS	RG	PG	R	-)	(RG	PS
27	RG	PG	R	-)	(RG	PS	RG	PG	R	-	G	P	G	R	S	-
28	G	-	G	R	S	-	N̲	P̲	R	-	G	P	G	R	S	-
29	G	-	G	R	S	-	N̲	P̲	R	-	G	P	G	R	S	-
Taan 5 30	PR	GP	NP	G	SR	GP	NŜ	R̂	RG	RS	GP	GR	G	GR	G	GR
Play Gat 3 times to end 31	G	-	G	R	S	-	N̲	P̲	R	-	G	P	G	R	S	-
32	G	-	G	R	S	-	N̲	P̲	R	-	G	P	G	R	S	-
33	G	-	G	R	S	-	N̲	P̲	R	-	G	P	G	R	S	-

Exercise 24: Raga Hansadhwani (Elaborated notation) – Indian Convention

RIDDHI SANYAL

Sheet Music has been created as well for the Raga **Hansadhwani**. The notation has been created considering the beginner student. Both the Indian & western notation depicts same composition of the Raga. After playing the same Alaap, you may start the sheet music for Raga Hansadhwani in Tintaal.

RAGA HAMSADWANI

Bandish, Antara and Few Taan

- Composed by Sri D. Madhusudan, Riddhi Sanyal

Sheet Music 22: Raga Hansadhwani - Western Convention Page 1

RIDDHI SANYAL

Sheet Music 23: Raga Hansadhwani - Western Convention Page 2

Day 43 to Day 46 – Raga Durga

Until now, during our journey on Classical, we have practiced the Raga Hansadhwani. It will be ideal to play Raga Durga now. The missing notes in Raga Hansadhwani are ma (m) and Dha (D). We will play more on ma (m) and Dha (D) now in Raga Durga whereas notes Ga (G) and Ni (N) are not present.

- ✓ It contains only 5 notes out of 7
- ✓ All are major notes, no flat / sharp

- ✓ Both side (to play upward / downward direction) are open to play
- ✓ This Raga is suitable to play in Flute more than string instruments
- ✓ As discussed, it's the most suitable Raga to learn after starting with Hansadhwani as it covers the missing notes from Hansadhwani.

Direction and Notes to Play:

Upward - *Arohana*					
Indian	S	R	m	P	D	Ŝ
Western	C	D	F	G	A	C'

Table 7: Raga Durga – Upward direction / Arohana

Downward - *Avarohana*					
Indian	Ŝ	D	P	m	R	S
Western	C'	A	G	F	D	C

Table 8: Raga Durga – Downward direction / Avarohana

Timings of Playing Raga Durga: Second quarter of night (9pm to 12 am). However, you may learn / practice at your suitable time.

Thaat: Bilaval

Vadi / **Primary Note**:	D	(A in western)
Samavadi / **Secondary Note**:	R	(D in western)

Chalan / *Pakad* / **Progression of Notes**: D S, R m P D, m P D P, m R m P.

Alaap:

S ... Ḍ S ... Ḍ P ... P Ḍ S ...

Ḍ S R ... m R . m R S ...

S R m P ... R m R P ... m R S ...

R m P D ... m P D ... P D . m P . R m . S R m P D ...

P D Ŝ D ... P Ḍ S Ḍ .. Ḍ S R m R ... m P D ,,,

R m P D ... m P D Ŝ ... R̂ Ŝ ...

R̂ ṁ R̂ Ŝ ... D P m P ... D P m R ... R m R S ... Ḍ S

RIDDHI SANYAL

Bandish, few *Taan*, Final *Tihai* to practice in Teentaal:

Tabla Bol >>	(0) Na	Tin	Tin	Ta	TeTe	Dhin	Dhin	Dha	(+) Dha	Dhin	Dhin	Dha	Dha	Dhin	Dhin	Dha		
Raga Section	Time Sig	1	2	3	4	5	6	7	8	9	10	11	12	13	14	15	16	Times to play	Return to Sig
Bandish	①	S	R	m	P	D	P	m	P	D	-	m	P	m	R	S	-	2	
	3	S	Ḍ	S	R	m	-	R	m	P	-	D	P	m	R	S	-	2	① - 1
Antara	7	m	R	m	P	D	-	P	D	Ŝ	-	Ŝ	Ř	Ŝ	D	P	m	1	
	8	m	R	m	P	D	-	P	D	Ŝ	-	Ŝ	-	D	Ř	Ŝ	-	2	
	10	D	-	P	D	P	m	R	m	P	-	m	P	m	R	S	-	2	① - 1
Taan 1	14									SR	m	Rm	P	DP	mP	mR	S	1	
	15	(SR	mP	D)	(SR	mP	D)	(SR	mP									1	① - 9
Taan 2	18	SḌ	S	RS	R	mR	m	Pm	P	DP	D	Pm	P	Rm	P	mR	S	2	① - 1
Taan 3	21	R	SR	mP	D	Rm	PD	Pm	R	SḌ	:P	ḌS	R	SR	mP	mR	S	2	① - 1
Taan 4	24									RS	ḌS	R	SR	mP	DP	m	Rm	1	
	25	PD	P	m	Rm	Pm	RP	mR	S	(SR	mP	D	mP	D	-)	(SR	mP	1	
	26	D	mP	D	-)	(SR	mP	D	mP									1	① - 9
Taan 5	29									mP	DR	mP	DP	DŜ	DP	mP	DP	1	
	30	mR	SR	mP	DP	Rm	RP	mR	S	mP	DR	mP	DP	DŜ	DP	mP	DP	1	
	31	mR	SR	mP	DP	Rm	RP	mR	S	(RS	mR	Pm	DP	D	-)	(RS	mR	1	
	32	Pm	DP	D	-)	(RS	mR	Pm	DP									1	① - 9
Tihai 6	35									(ŜŜ	ŜD	DD	PP	Pm	mm	RR	S)	1	
	36	(ŜŜ	ŜD	DD	PP	Pm	mm	RR	S)	(ŜŜ	ŜD	DD	PP	Pm	mm	RR	S)	1	
	37	(mR	mP	D)	(mR	mP	D)	(mR	mP									1	① - 9

Exercise 26: Raga Durga − Indian Convention

The 1st, 2nd & 3rd *Taan*s are composed in such a way that it will suite a Flute player to take breath at regular interval. It will be ideal to take breath during the single notes in the Taan. Gradually 4th and 5th Taan are set to overcome little hurdle.

Learners should learn to play each Taan individually first. Play for 20 – 30 times. After gaining confidence and maintaining same tempo, you may play with Teental.

RIDDHI SANYAL

You may play few more Taan before finishing. To compose new Taan, it can be with or without Tihai. Example, 2nd & 3rd Taans are without Tihai. They start from 1st beat and end at 16th beat. They are merging with Bandish at "① – 1". If you want to introduce Tihai along with Taan, it will be more appropriate to merge at Sam "① – 9" with the Bandish. Examples are 1st, 4th and 5th Taan. It's all mathematical calculation to arrive the number of notes in a Taan. Initially, for first few months, you have to follow the written Taan, but gradually you should try to play Taan dynamically from your mind. Final Tihai (No 6) is prepared to conclude the Raga.

RIDDHI SANYAL

RAGA DURGA

Bandish, Antara and Few Taan — Composed by Sri D. Madhusudan, *Riddhi Sanyal*

Sheet Music 24: Raga Durga — Western Convention, Page 1

RIDDHI SANYAL

Sheet Music 25: Raga Durga – Western Convention, Page 2

RIDDHI SANYAL

Sheet Music 26: Raga Durga – Western Convention, Page 3

Day 47 to Day 50 – Raga Bilaval

Bilaval (also termed as *Bilawal*) is the Raga with the name of the Thaat Bilaval. It's the most basic Raga with the presence of all major notes. Compared to western, Bilaval is equivalent to Ionian mode with all major notes. Carnatic equivalent of Bilaval Raga is *Dheerasankarabharanam*.

Direction and Notes to Play:

Upward - *Arohana*							
Indian	S	R	G	m	P	D	N	Ŝ
Western	C	D	E	F	G	A	B	C'

Table 9: Raga Bilaval – Upward direction / Arohana

Downward - *Avarohana*							
Indian	Ŝ	N	D	P	m	G	R	S
Western	C'	B	A	G	F	E	D	C

Table 10: Raga Bilaval – Downward direction / Avarohana

Timings: Morning 6AM to 9AM
Vadi | **Primary Note:**   **D**   (A in western)
Samavadi | **Secondary Note:**   **G**   (E in western)

Chalan | *Pakad* | **Progression of Notes**: S R G m, m G m, G P D N Ŝ, Ŝ N D P, m P m G, G m R S.

Alaap:

S ... R S N̲ S ... N̲ D P ... D̲ N S ...

S R G ... G m R S ... R G P ... G P D P ... m R S ...

R G P ... P D N D P ... m G P ... D P . N D P ...

P ... D N D P ... m P D . P ... G P D N Ŝ ... R̂ Ĝ R̂ Ŝ ...

Ŝ N D ... N D . D P ... m P m G R ... m R S ...

Exercise 27: Rag Bilaval - Alaap

Bandish, Antara, Taan to practice in Teentaal:

The Bandish, Antara and the Taans are created for Rag Bilaval considering for the beginner students. Taan 3, Taan 4, Taan 5 – each can be played 2 times with Taal as mentioned. Finally, you can conclude the play by playing the Bandish 3 times.

Tabla Bol >>		(0) Na	Tin	Tin	Ta	TeTe	Dhin	Dhin	Dha	(+) Dha	Dhin	Dhin	Dha	Dha	Dhin	Dhin	Dha		
Raga Section	Time Sig	1	2	3	4	5	6	7	8	9	10	11	12	13	14	15	16	Times to play	Return toS
Bandish	①	m	G	R	G	-	P	D	N	Ŝ	-	N	D	P	m	G	-	2	
	3	m	R	-	S	R	G	P	m	G	P	m	G	m	R	S	-	2	① 1
Antara	7	P	m	G	P	D	-	N	-	Ŝ	-	Ŝ	-	R̂	N	Ŝ		2	
	9	N	D	-	P	m	P	m	G	P	-	m	G	m	R	S		2	① 1
Taan 1	13									SR	Gm	PD	NŜ	ND	Pm	GR	S	1	
Tihai 1	14	(GP	DN	Ŝ)	(GP	DN	Ŝ)	(GP	DN									1	① 9
Taan 2	17	RS	RG	PD	NŜ	ND	Pm	GR	S	(RS	RG	P	DN	Ŝ	-)	(RS	RG	1	
Taan 2	18	P	DN	Ŝ	-)	(RS	RG	P	DN									1	① 9
Taan 3	21	GR	Gm	GP	DN	ŜN	DP	mG	m	GR	Gm	GP	DN	ŜN	DP	Gm	RS	2	① 1
Taan 4	25	Gm	RS	RG	PD	ND	P	Gm	P	DN	ŜR̂	ŜN	DP	DP	mG	mR	S	2	① 1
Taan 5	29	mR	SR	GP	mG	PD	N	ŜN	DP	mP	D	ND	P	Gm	P	Gm	RS	2	① 1

Exercise 28: Rag Bilaval - Indian Convention

RIDDHI SANYAL

RAGA BILAWAL

Bandish, Antara and Few Taan

- Composed by Sri D. Madhusudan, Riddhi Sanyal

Sheet Music 27: Rag Bilaval - Western Convention, Page 1

RIDDHI SANYAL

Sheet Music 28: Rag Bilaval - Western Convention, Page 2

Day 51 to Day 54 – Raga Mand

Raga Mand has been originated from Rajasthan and it's in Indian Classical music since more than 500 years. Melodious Songs has been composed on this Raga specifically *Vaishnab Bhajans, Miraji's Bhajans, Kirtans, Ramprasadi Bhajans,* Tagore Songs etc.

All notes of Mand Raga are major notes. Progression of Mand will remind you 2 Ragas. During upward direction, Raga Durga will be followed and during downward direction, Raga Bilawal will be followed. That means, during upward direction 2 notes are not played – G and N. While descending, all notes are played. From the previous lessons, we are already comfortable playing both Ragas Durga & Bilawal, now it will be ideal to learn Raga Mand.

Direction and Notes to Play:

RIDDHI SANYAL

Upward - *Arohana*						
Indian	S	R	m	P	D	Ŝ
Western	C	D	F	G	A	C'

Table 11: Raga Mand – Upward direction / Arohana

Downward - *Avarohana*							
Indian	Ŝ	N	D	P	m	G	R	S
Western	C'	B	A	G	F	E	D	C

Table 12: Raga Mand – Downward direction / Avarohana

Timings: Night 9PM to 12PM
***Vadi* | Primary Note:**   S   (C in western)
***Samavadi* | Secondary Note:**   P   (G in western)
Thaat: Bilawal
***Chalan* | *Pakad* | Progression of Notes:** S R m G R, m P D, Ḍ S R S, m G R S, P D Ŝ
Ṟ, Ŝ N D P, P D P m G R S.

Alaap:

     S ... Ṉ Ḍ S ... Ṉ Ḍ P̱ ... P̱ Ḍ S ...
     S R m ... G R ... m G R S
     R m G R ... m P m G R ... R m P D P ... m P D P m G R S...
     S R m P D ... m G R m P D... D Ŝ N D ... Ŝ ...
     Ŝ Ṟ Ŝ ... Ŝ Ṟ Ŝ N D ... P D Ŝ...
     Ŝ N D ... D P m P ... m P m G R ... R m G R S ...

Exercise 29: Rag Mand - Alaap

Bandish, Antara, Taan to practice in Teentaal:

Raga Mand can be played at various instruments. In our *Gharana*, we have observed Violin, Mandolin, Sarod, Banjo, Guitar and as well as Flute players to play Mand Raga. Below sections of Raga - *Bandish, Taan, Bistar* are specifically created for Flute players. Flute players will get plenty of opportunity to take breath in between playing the Bandish, Antara and various Taans.

Taan 4 is basically created as Raga *Bistar*. That means to elaborate the Raga notes taking more time. *Bistar* illustrates the Raga little bit more to all as it's goes slowly than the Taan.

RIDDHI SANYAL

Last part of the Raga is demonstrated with Tihai to conclude the Raga. Learners can get the idea, feel the rhythm and compose more Taan or Bistar the Raga with Tal. Tihai is not mandatory with each Taan or Bistar. If you are not giving Tihai, you have to complete the Taan / Bistar properly either at "① - 1" or "① - 9" position. During initial days of learning, we recommend students to follow each notes given in the exercise. After practicing the Raga & Taans for 30 – 40 times in one seating, you will automatically get ideas to develop your own Taan.

Tabla Bol >>		(0) Na	Tin	Tin	Ta	TeTe	Dhin	Dhin	Dha	(+) Dha	Dhin	Dhin	Dha	Dha	Dhin	Dhin	Dha		
Raga Section	Time Sig	1	2	3	4	5	6	7	8	9	10	11	12	13	14	15	16	Times to play	Return to Sig
Bandish	①	R	m	P	-	D	Ŝ	N	-	D	-	P	m	G	R	S	-	2	Next Section
	3	N̲	D̲	P̲	D̲	S	-	R	m	P	-	D	P	m	G	R	S	2	① - 1
Antara	7	P	m	G	R	-	m	P	D	Ŝ	-	Ŝ	R̂	Ŝ	N	D	P	1	
	8	P	m	G	R	-	m	P	D	Ŝ	-	Ŝ	-	R̂	D	Ŝ	-	1	
	9	D	Ŝ	R̂	-	ṁ	Ĝ	R̂	-	Ŝ	-	Ŝ	-	R̂	D	Ŝ	-	1	
	10	N	-	D	P	m	-	G	R	mP	DŜ	ND	Pm	GR	mG	RR	S	1	① - 1
Taan 1	13									SR	m	Rm	P	mP	DP	mG	RS	1	
	14	(SR	mP	D)	(SR	mP	D)	(SR	mP									1	① - 9
Taan 2	17									GR	mG	RP	mG	Rm	P	mG	RS	1	
	18	(GR	mP	D)	(GR	mP	D)	(GR	mP									1	① - 9
Taan 3	21									Rm	PD	Pm	PD	Ŝ	R̂Ŝ	ND	P	1	
	22	mG	Rm	GR	mP	D	Pm	GR	S	(Rm	GR	mP	DP	D	-)	(Rm	GR	1	
	23	mP	DP	D	-)	(Rm	GR	mP	DP									1	① - 9
Taan 4 / Bistar	26	R	m	-	-	GR	m	-	-	GR	m	-	-	Pm	G	-	-	2	Play (17,18) for 2 times
	27	Rm	P	-	-	mP	D	-	-	PD	Ŝ	ŜR̂	ŜN	DP	m	GR	S		
	28	ŜN	DŜ	DP	DP	mP	mR	mG	RS	(SR	mG	R)	(SR	mG	R)	(SR	mG	1	① - 1
Tihai 5	31									(ŜŜ	NN	DD	P	Rm	PN	Ŝ	-)	1	
	32	(ŜŜ	NN	DD	P	Rm	PN	Ŝ	-)	(ŜŜ	NN	DD	P	Rm	PN	Ŝ	-)	1	
Tihai 6	33	(Rm	mP	D)	(Rm	mP	D)	(Rm	mP									1	① - 9

Exercise 30: Raga Mand – Indian Convention

RIDDHI SANYAL

RAGA MAND

Bandish, Antara and Few Taan

— Composed by Sri D. Madhusudan, Riddhi Sanyal

Sheet Music 29: Raga Mand – Western Convention, Page 1

RIDDHI SANYAL

Sheet Music 30: Raga Mand – Western Convention, Page 2

RIDDHI SANYAL

Sheet Music 31: Raga Mand – Western Convention, Page 3

Day 55 to Day 59 – Raga Bhupali (also known as Bhopali / Bhoopali)

Until now, we have learnt Raga Hansadhwani, Raga Durga, Raga Bilaval and Raga Mand. Now it's time to move on to one of the sweetest Raga – Bhupali. Few basics and the reason for teaching Bhupali are

- ✓ It contains only 5 notes out of 7 (Pentatonic Scale)
- ✓ All are major notes, no flat / sharp
- ✓ Both side (to play upward / downward direction) are open to play, no restriction of notes
- ✓ This Raga is also suitable to play in Flute more than string instruments

North East is one of the hub of Indian Flutes as northeast states like Assam, Arunachal & Tripura naturally produce Bamboo trees from which best quality flutes are produced. We found similarity in North East music with Raga Bhupali. For example, Bihu Songs in Assam *"Bihure Logon Modhure Logon"* belongs to Raga Bhupali. One of the famous Bollywood song *"Dil Hoom Hoom Kare (Movie: Rudaali)"* belongs to Raga Bhupali which has been composed by Legendary singer & composer *Sri Bhupen Hazarika (from Assam)*. Another famous Bollywood song *"Kanchi Re Kanchi Re (Movie: Hare Rama Hare Krishna)"* was composed in Raga Bhupali and that depicts the music of Nepal and eastern Himalayas. We found plenty of flute applications in Bihu songs, the songs / music of eastern Himalaya and on Nepali songs.

Raga Bhupali is used for devotional songs as the melody brings *Bhakti Rasa*. For example, famous Bhakti Song from Jagjit Singh – *"He Govind, He Gopal, He Dayal"* is composed on Raga Bhupali.

Coming to the Raga Details, two notes are not used in Raga Bhupali – m and N. Rest 5 notes are used at both directions.

Direction and Notes to Play:

RIDDHI SANYAL

Upward - *Arohana*						
Indian	S	R	G	P	D	Ŝ
Western	C	D	E	G	A	C'

Table 13: Raga Bhupali – Upward direction / Arohana

Downward - *Avarohana*						
Indian	Ŝ	D	P	G	R	S
Western	C'	A	G	E	D	C

Table 14: Raga Bhupali – Downward direction / Avarohana

Timings: Night 6PM to 9PM
Vadi / **Primary Note**:   G (E in western)
Samavadi / **Secondary Note**: D (A in western)
Thaat: Kalyan
Chalan / *Pakad* / **Progression of Notes**: S R G R S, D̲ S R G, P̲ D̲ S R G, G R G P D Ŝ, Ŝ D P, P D P G R S.

Alaap:

S ... D̲ S R ... S R G R S ... S D̲ P ... P̲ D̲ S R G ...
S R G R G P ... G P D P ... P G R S . R G ...
P̲ D̲ S R G . R G P ... D P G R ... G P ...
G P D . Ŝ D P ... P D Ŝ ...
Ŝ R̂ Ŝ ... Ŝ R̂ Ĝ R̂ Ŝ ... Ŝ D P ... P D Ŝ...
Ŝ D P ... G P D P ... G R G... G R S ...

Exercise 31: Rag Bhupali - Alaap

***Bandish, Antara, Taan* to practice in Teentaal:**
Considering beginner flutist, the following Raga Bandish and related sections are created. Flutist will get time intervals to take breath in between the entire notes. During Bandish and Antara, there are plenty of positions to help you taking breath. Ex: during the 1st line of Bandish, you can take breath at 2nd, 10th and at the last positions. Similarly, at Antara 1st line, you can take breath at 3rd, 6th, 10th, 12th, and at the last. In case of Taan, you have to take small breath just after playing the single

RIDDHI SANYAL

notes. Ex: At Taan 1, take breath at position 16th just after playing S. During each Tihai, you can take breath after the last note. Sometimes you may not need to take the breath. Then it's ok to play as long as you can play continuously without distorting the frequency of the notes of the Octave.

It's always recommended to play first line of the Bandish for 2 times or more. Considering 'Times To Play', the Time Signatures have been created. Taan 4 is actually created to showcase how you can elaborate (*Bistar*) on some specific notes of the Raga. To make it clearly readable, all Tihai have been surrounded by the bracket symbols '(' and to end ')'. At the end, 2 Tihai have been given and one after another can be played to conclude the Raga. Within this small span of learning, you will get to know few Tihai patterns and to return to Bandish after the end of Tihai –

- 3 Beat Tihai (3 x 3 = 9 beats) – used in Taan 1, Taan 2, Tihai 6
- 6 Beat Tihai (6 x 3 = 18 beats)– used in Taan 3
- 8 Beat Tihai (8 x 3 = 24 beats) – used in Tihai 5

Tabla Bol >>		(0) Na	Tin	Tin	Ta	TeTe	Dhin	Dhin	Dha	(+) Dha	Dhin	Dhin	Dha	Dha	Dhin	Dhin	Dha		
Raga Section	Time Sig	1	2	3	4	5	6	7	8	9	10	11	12	13	14	15	16	Time s to play	Return to Sig
Bandish	①	Ŝ	-	D	P	G	R	S	R	G	-	G	P	G	R	S	-	2	Next Section
	3	S	D̲	S	R	G	-	G	P	R	G	-	P	G	R	S	-	2	①-1
Antara	7	P	G	-	P	G	-	P	D	Ŝ	-	Ŝ	-	Ĝ	R̂	Ŝ	-	2	
	9	Ŝ	D	Ŝ	R̂	Ŝ	D	-	P	R	G	-	P	G	R	S	-	2	①-1
Taan 1	13									SR	GP	DŜ	DP	RG	PR	GR	S	1	
	14	(SR	GR	G)	(SR	GR	G)	(SR	GR									1	①-9
Taan 2	17									RG	P	DŜ	DP	RG	P	GR	S	1	
	18	(RS	SR	G)	(RS	SR	G)	(RS	SR									1	①-9
Taan 3	21									GR	SG	RS	GP	DP	GP	GR	S	1	
	22	D̲S	RD̲	SR	GP	DŜ	DP	GR	S	(GR	S	RG	PR	G	-)	(GR	S	1	
	23	RG	PR	G	-)	(GR	S	RG	PR									1	①-9
Taan 4 / Bistar	26	SR	G	-	-	SR	G	-	-	RG	P	-	-	PD	PR	GR	S	2	
	28	RG	P	SR	GP	D	-	-	-	GP	D	RG	PD	Ŝ	-	-	-	1	
	29	ŜR̂	Ŝ	PD	ŜR̂	Ĝ	-	-	-	ŜD	ŜR̂	ŜD	PR	GP	DP	GR	S	1	①-1
Tihai 5	32									(ŜŜ	DD	PP	GG	RR	GP	GR	S)	1	
Tihai 5	33	(ŜŜ	DD	PP	GG	RR	GP	GR	S)	(ŜŜ	DD	PP	GG	RR	GP	GR	S)	1	
Tihai 6	34	(RG	RP	G)	(RG	RP	G)	(RG	RP									1	①-9

Exercise 32: Raga Bhupali – Indian Convention

RIDDHI SANYAL

RAGA BHUPALI

Bandish, Antara and Few Taan

- Composed by Sri D. Madhusudan, Riddhi Sanyal

Sheet Music 32: Raga Bhupali – Western Convention, Page 1

RIDDHI SANYAL

Sheet Music 33: Raga Bhupali – Western Convention, Page 2

RIDDHI SANYAL

Tihai 6   D.C. al Fine

Sheet Music 34: Raga Bhupali – Western Convention, Page 3

Day 60 – Recap, Further learning steps

The 3rd phase / section of learning is completely on Indian Classical Raga.

- ✓ We have learnt to play the Bandish and taans on –
  - o Raga Hansadhwani
  - o Raga Durga
  - o Raga Bilaval
  - o Raga Mand
  - o Raga Bhupali
- ✓ Now we have idea on the Tintal – 16 beat rhythm. Raga gets its complete identity and impression with the help of Tintal.
- ✓ We are gradually learning the Tihai at the end of Taan to merge with the Bandish again.
- ✓ It's nice to learn and play the Alaap before playing the Raga in Taal.

Next steps will be a course of learning with balance in various Songs and Indian Classical Ragas. These are the ways for the learner to continue the journey –

- ❖ To learn from Guru to improve your skills
- ❖ To learn the depth of Indian Classical Ragas
- ❖ To understand more on the Taal / rhythm
- ❖ To learn to prepare your own Taan & Tihai
- ❖ To start with the following Ragas with continuation with current –
  - o Raga Yaman (Thaat Kalyan)
  - o Raga Kafi (Thaat Kafi)
  - o Raga Brindavani Sarang (Thaat Kafi)
  - o Raga Khamaj (Thaat Khamaj)
  - o Raga Desh (Thaat Khamaj)
  - o Raga Tilong (Thaat Khamaj)
  - o Raga Megh (Thaat Kafi)
- ❖ To learn various songs, semi-classical music, songs related to specific ragas.
- ❖ Need to learn how to play with a group of musicians.
- ❖ To understand the chord of the music and classical raga.

Feel free to connect with Author to continue your learning in music.

RIDDHI SANYAL

11.0   Image Gallery

Photo Gallery 1: With Guruji after a successful function

RIDDHI SANYAL

Photo Gallery 2: Guruji on Flute with a different mood / bhaba

Photo Gallery 3: Playing Raga Puriya Kalyan on a Function at E scale

RIDDHI SANYAL

Photo Gallery 4: Guruji with students in a street function

RIDDHI SANYAL

Photo Gallery 5: Our Music director - Guruji in Banjo

Photo Gallery 6: On Beniyasakala's Annual Function

Photo Gallery 7: At the Temple of Lahiri Mahasaya. Accompanying Guruji & Krishnendu

RIDDHI SANYAL

Photo Gallery 8: Guruji & students at the bank of Ganga River, near Belur math, Howrah

Photo Gallery 9: Beniyasahakala Orchestra - Function on 1999, before the digital age

RIDDHI SANYAL

Photo Gallery 10: Street Function at Dashashwamedh Ghat, Varanasi, 2017

Photo Gallery 11: Recording moments

RIDDHI SANYAL

12.0   Improvisation of Classical Flute to 8 Hole

Guruji, Sri D. Madhusudan is an innovator & practitioner on 8-hole Hindustani Flute. This is an innovative idea to bring Flute one more level up in Classical journey. Apart from the 6 holes, one hole is created to block by left hand thumb. This brings the note Pa in the same breath force of S R G m. The added advantage is that, you can smoothly raise the sound to Pa from S R G m. Like

- m P
- G P
- M P
- R P

Photo Gallery 12: Comparing 6 Hole and 8 Hole Flutes (E Scale). 8-Hole is the dark one.
Whereas in the 6 Hole, it's not possible to smoothly raise the notes to Pa since, Pa comes in higher breath force.

RIDDHI SANYAL

Therefore, the note Pa can be played by Left thumb now.

Photo Gallery 13: Playing P (Pa) using Left Thumb in 8 Hole Flute

Now the questions is what will happen on the flow of the P D or P N since P is now in lower breath force and D is in higher breath force.

To overcome that, there is another hole created to be played with right hand little finger.

Photo Gallery 14: Playing n (Komal / Flat ni) in 8 Hole Flute

Summarizing the differences of SARGAM in 8 hole Flute (w.r.t. Scale C) –
- Lower P̲ (G4) - All Fingers Blocked
- Lower D̲ (A4) - Lift RH Little finger
- Lower n̠ (A#4 / Bb4)– Lift RH Ring & Little fingers
- Lower N̠ (B4) - Lift RH Middle, Ring & Little fingers
- Middle S (C5) - Lift all RH fingers
- Middle R, G, m, M are same with addition, LH thumb to block the lower Hole

RIDDHI SANYAL

- Middle P (G5) - Lift the left thumb. So all holes are open this time.
- Another way to play P (G5), block all finger and blow higher.
- Middle D and onwards - Blow with more force at same finger position as mentioned above.

Photo Gallery 15: Practicing 8 Hole Flute (E Scale)

So now, you can understand that to play P D, P N, P Ŝ and so on, the note P should be played with all fingers blocked and blow higher. Same Pa will be played by lifting thumb when playing M P, m P, G P and so on.

One more note is added in this Flute. That is the Higher P (G6). It can be played by lifting the thumb with higher force.

Best suited Ragas for 8 Hole Flute are **Yaman, Yaman Kalyan, Puriya Kalyan, Kedar, Miyan Mallar, Shiva Ranjani, Pilu, Bihag, Yog** etc. Smooth raising and blending with P will add a new effect than 6 hole flute.

The learning and teaching of 8 Hole Flute are only for the advanced students who are comfortable with 6 hole base E flute already. This is an innovation of Guruji's lessons starting from making of 8-hole Flute to end-to-end teaching. It is doubtful

RIDDHI SANYAL

whether you will get 8-hole Hindustani flute in market. Truly interested candidates may contact author and then suitable flutes can be provisioned for the students.

*** *Please note that, the 8-hole Flute discussed above is not to be compared with Carnatic Flute / Venu. Both are different in look and playing style.*

13.0   Instrumental Workshop & Recent Performances

2017 March, Varanasi, Musical Gathering

With our beloved Guruji, we have visited Varanasi for 3-4 days. Overall group has almost 20 people with around 15 musicians. During our visit, one of our primary objective was to perform at the Dasaswamedh Ghat. After the evening *Ganga Arati*, around 8pm, we started playing. There were around 6-7 Flutists, 2-3 Guitarists, 2-3 Mandolin players, 2 Violin players. Off course, Guruji, who overall guided & directed, played sometimes Flute, Guitar to provide balance in the music and visiting crowd. Variety of music played, starting from light classical to Bollywood songs. Musicians took a circular space in the benches of the Ghats. Almost 70 - 100 People surrounding us formed larger circle, standing on upstairs of Ghats. It was a nice ambiance and everyone enjoyed the music and requesting for songs of their choices.

One of the morning in Varanasi, together we were planning to visit Yogiraj *Sri Shyama Charan Lahiri Mahasaya's* Temple. The temple opens at 10:30 am. *Sri Shyama Charan Lahiri Mahasaya*, better known as *Lahiri Mahasaya* or *Lahiri Baba*, was Kriya Yoga Master, Sadguru, during 19th century at Varanasi. He has attained the highest state of Spiritual Realization by practicing Kriya Yoga. He and his disciples have given *diksha* (Initiation) on the Kriya Yoga to thousands of needy people in entire world. For all Yogis, in any religion, the temple of *Sri Lahiri Mahasaya* is a precious & sacred place.

The temple is a little tricky to reach from the main road. You have to enter into the small lanes of Varanasi. Walking towards Dasaswamedh Ghat from Godowlia, you have to take right before the Ghat into a small lane. After walking 8-10 minutes, you will reach after asking for Lahiri Mahasaya's temple. You can visit from the Ghats too. From Dasaswamedh Ghat, take right walk until Chausathi ghat. Enter the Chausathi ghat, climb the stairs of Ghat. Then walk for 2-3 minutes to reach the temple.

With Guruji's inspiration, we all assembled there by 10:45 pm. There Guruji, Krishnendu and myself had played Raga Jog inside the temple premises seating area. We played with the base flute E with the Tanpura on Mobile. This was a complete different experience to play in a temple of pin drop silence. Raga Jog was named to connect your soul to supreme. Guruji has chosen the Raga Jog in front of Yogiraj Sri Lahiri Mahasaya. It was a perfect honor to Yogiraj, the Kriya Yoga Master from us.

RIDDHI SANYAL

Most of us were in the state of Dhana after playing or listening to the voice of flute with Raga Joga. It was a peaceful and divine experience.

While returning from temple around 12, we took the small lane towards Dasaswamedh Ghat. There is a Lassi shop with Bamboo finishing. We all gathered in the lassi shop. Guruji asked us to open the instruments and we all played one of the Guruji's famous composition - Isti Kutum - voice of bird. Nice experience playing flute inside the bamboo covered restaurant and very good ambiance there. People over there enjoyed and participated with claps.

During night, we had the similar street performance. A TV Channel from Lucknow was there to record the Ghat areas. They found interesting street function and started recording our videos. Then on their request, we all played "Vandemataram" and that concluded for the day.

Overall, it was a peaceful & delightful musical experience at Varanasi for all of us.

2017 Aug, Bangalore: Musical Workshop, Street Performance & Organized Grand Function:

Overview: The hosts of this workshop were Sri Palash Taru Guha and Smt Arundhati Mitra on the school premises of Sri Setu & Vinitha Mahadevan. Mr. Palash is a bosom friend of our Guruji and Palash Sir is also an expert flutist. The idea of the workshop was to provide a demo & illustration of variety of instruments to the pre-registered learner / students. They will be able to see the instruments, feel it, and try to play it one by one. The initial guidance of playing can be given to the participants. Once spend time of at least 1 hour with each instrument, finally the learners can decide what instrument to learn.

Venue of the workshop: *Rag Ragini Kalakhetra*, Sai Colony, Kadugodi. Bangalore (Landmark *Manu Residency, Kadugodi*).

This time, Guruji has taken 4 of us with him to attend a workshop and to perform in the function.

- ➢ Krishnendu, Sourish and myself for the Flute
- ➢ Partha with Violin, Mandolin
- ➢ Sourish with Banjo
- ➢ Additionally, I had Harmonica, Melodica, and Synth to accompany.
- ➢ Organizer has arranged Synthesizer & Guitar there itself.

Day1: 11th Aug, Friday: Journey Day: Our journey was planned from Kolkata (HWH) to Bangalore (YPR) via Duranta Exp. One good thing about the train Duranta, is that it's not stop train. During the onward journey, when so many musicians are together with instruments, we were obviously started playing since morning. After lunch, Guruji assigned us one task. He was carrying around 45 Flutes. Those were required

RIDDHI SANYAL

to be fine-tuned and to be marked with proper scale. 3 of us started that activity with the guidance from Guruji. Activities are like - sharping the holes of flutes, removing the small particles / dusts, washing with water, playing all notes on the flute to find whether all notes are correct, etc. On our report, Guruji used to correct that note with a small knife like toolkit. Finally, our job was to mark the flute with its scale. Those were mostly beginner flutes with scales varying from C, C#, D, B, Bb and few for advanced students on the scale of F#, G, G# etc. It was a nice time spend during the onward journey and with full of activity & play music.

Day2: 12ᵗʰ Aug: Reached Bangalore: The journey continued and we reached 2 hours delayed at Yeshwantpur Station, Bangalore around 6 pm. Hosts have provided the on call cab and we reached the venue by next 1 hour. They have arranged the stay at Manu Residency, which is the nearer landmark to the music academy. Just after getting fresh, within the next hour, we have visited the host's place. We received the welcome drink of green tea that was really needed at that time. The homely ambiance was so good, we automatically started playing Raga Yaman in that beautiful evening. Palash Sir also joined us playing flute. After 30 minutes of playing, we received the Green Tea again which was splendid.

Day3: 13th Aug, Sunday: The Workshop Day: The workshop timings were 9:30 am – 1:30 pm. 5 different rooms are arranged - one for vocal, one for Flute / Bansuri, one for Guitar, Keyboard, one for Violin, Mandolin & Banjo and the last room for percussion instruments with Tabla & Mridangam. Before staring the workshop, Guruji inaugurated the occasion with lighting the holy lamp and the students sang the Ganesh Bandana. Guruji, Krishnendu and I were present in the Flute section. On Guruji's request, a short history of flute as a classical instrument and life of Pt. Pannalal Ghosh were presented to the learners.

From the huge bag with full of 50 flutes, we had removed all of them and whichever was suitable to the learners, it was given to them individually for the start / practice. The notation of SRGmPDNS were demonstrated to them. Slowly they were playing the first note - m then G, R, S ... Most of them were able to play the notes with good quality sound. Some of them were able to completely SRGmPDNS notes. That was a gift to us when the learner was able to play complete notes on the very the first day of holding flute. Total participants of the workshop were around 35 - 40. All of them were given a chance to participate in the flute section.

Additionally, I had given the demo of Mouth Organ / Harmonica to the learners on how to play the SRGmPDNS & illustrated with light music and songs.

The other rooms were also a full success where participants were able to see, hold the Mandolin, Guitar, Banjo, Tabla and learned the basics. We had limited number of

RIDDHI SANYAL

String instruments and so learners were given chance to play one by one. Hence, every 12-15 learners moved from one room to another after 45 minutes to 1 hour.

In the while, Guruji started a live function on Raga *Brindavani Sarang* with Tabla Teacher Sri Arnab. That happened outside the demo rooms in the assemble area of the academy.

Overall, the workshop was innovative and this kind of workshop is only feasible with the knowledgeable master like Guruji. That is the only place where every learner can make the link to all possible musical instruments in the journey.

Day4:14thAug, Monday: Rehearsal Day: There was a pre-planned function organized by Hosts. Several singers were planning to perform along with us and we had to support on the background music. I moved to play both Synth and Flute and as on need basis with the singers. Guruji was sometimes on Flute and sometimes on Guitar. There was one interesting performance with Raga Melody based on the 12-15 Ragas and corresponding Golden Era Hindi songs. First Guruji played the Flute on the Raga accompanied by several String instruments & Piano. Then 10-12 chorus singers started on the corresponding song. The continued for 2 minutes on the song and then again Guruji started the next Raga.

Apart from rehearsals, whenever we got time, Palash Sir & Guruji started playing for various Ragas. During various time of day & night they are on Raga Bairagi, Bageshree, Pilu, Bhimpalas, Marwa, etc. We tried to accompany as much time permits.

Day5: 15th Aug, Tuesday: Independence Day - Function Day:

Street Music near Whitefield Station: Inspired by Guruji, we all get ready and went out for a walk with our instruments. On route to Whitefield station, there was an auto stand under the flyover. Around 10am, we saw that someone has already hosted the flag. Near the flag, Guruji asked us to stand. We opened the instruments. Sourish on Banjo, Partha on Violin, Krishnendu on Flute, Guruji on Guitar / Flute and myself on Flute & Harmonica as per need. We played the patriotic songs like *Sare Jahan Se Accha*, *Vandemataram*, etc. We also played few compositions from Guruji like March Music, folk music like *Istikutum* etc. We have played for 30-40 minutes. People were listening & appreciating a lot. It's an exchange of culture on the precious Independence day. The auto drivers on the stand came and organized Tea and snacks for us.

After spending time with the local people over there, we visited the Whitefield station, and played the similar songs near to Whitefield station. There also people enjoyed and appreciated.

Grand Function: It was planned in the evening 5:30 pm. Auditorium inside a Flat complex was booked by the Hosts. I had to play Synth continuously until all of the singers performed individually and in chorus. The Raga Melody went superb. Guruji was leading with Flute, controlling the rhythm, tempo and the duration of the songs on the corresponding Ragas.

RIDDHI SANYAL

After all singers, they honored Guruji to perform the concert on Classical Raga. We were playing the ***Raga Megh*** together on Flute, Violin with Tabla. It was a wonderful experience to everyone present there to listen to the 1-hour concert. After that, we played some light music to balance the Raga ambiance. The program ended around 8:30pm. It was still heavily raining outside since last 2 hours. We could imagine the consequence of *Raga Megh* played by multiple players.

Day6: 16th Aug, Wednesday: REST Day: It was complete rest day after the function as our return was on next day. We walked the surrounding parks, played music in the park. With Guruji, it is always only music, nothing else.

Day7: 17th Aug, Thursday: Return Journey: Our Ticket was on early morning around 9 am from Yeshwantpur (YPR) to Howrah in Duranta Exp. We started from the hotel very early at 6:30 am to avoid traffics in Bangalore and comfortably reached by 8am. Had breakfast in the station. Weather was as usual very much pleasant at Bangalore with mild colder breeze. On the station itself, Guruji had started playing morning Ragas. We joined as usual.

Train was on time. This time Guruji started composing new music. Half a line or one line he played, and then update the notation in a piece of paper. Once he completed the one musical piece, Renigunta station was crossed. He simply named that musical notation with the Station Renigunta. We all practiced the notation.

Total he has completed 4 Musical compositions in our journey and inspired us to practice those during the journey. Any improvisation needed was directly done upon our playing.

Day8: 18th Aug: Destination Home: Next day we reached Kolkata in the evening as the train was late for 2 hours again.

Lot of memories from Workshop, Street function, grand function, music compositions and overall a complete musical journey from the start to end. It was endless and unforgettable joy for all of music lovers like us.

RIDDHI SANYAL

14.0   Flute and Meditation

Indian Classical Music has been originated to offer songs, *Kheyals*, **Ragas**, *Kirtans*, chanting to lord. Offering Raga is one of the purest way to pray in front of God irrespective of the religion. Singing or playing music needs a deep concentration level of mind, as your mind has to perform at least 3-4 simultaneous actions –

1. Playing the music

2. Follow the rhythm or Taal

3. Listening the overall outcome.

4. Reading the Notation

Objective of practicing Ragas is simple and straight forward - to connect with God and offer the prayers to God. Comparing other instruments, Flute has the additional advantage in playing Raga that brings a Flute player closer to perform meditation. To play Flute, one has to hold the breath for say 15 - 20 seconds or more and side by side has to exhale the breath at a very slow and constant pace. Comparing to meditation, there also you have to perform aerobic exercise to improve per breathing cycle to 20, 30 seconds or more.

We have performed the study of a flute player and a yoga person performing meditation.

The observations are listed in below table –

Category / Parameters to Observe	Meditation	Singing / Playing Raga in any Indian classical instruments and additional advantage of Flute
Offering / Purpose	Meditation is the way of self-realization and it's the way to connect one-self with Supreme Soul / God. Hence meditation is always offered for connecting with God.	Indian Classical music is developed to offer songs, *Kheyals*, ragas, *Kirtans*, chanting to lord. Objective of practicing Ragas is simple and straight forward - to connect with God and offer the prayers to God.
Concentration	Techniques of meditation improves the concentration level of human mind.	Singing or playing music needs a deep concentration level of mind, as your mind has to perform 3-4 simultaneous actions as mentioned above.

RIDDHI SANYAL

Seating Duration & Posture	To practice *Dhyana*, one has to seat in a static posture for long duration, such as 30 minutes to 2/3 hours. The posture may be *Padmasana* or *Sidhyasana* or recommended by your Gurudeb / Master.	Flute players has to seat in a static posture for long time. To follow any asana like *Sidhyasana*, will help the player to seat for longer duration like 30 minutes to 2 hours. Always follow Gurudeb / master for the seating recommended posture for you. Posture of flutist is almost static, except the finger movements.
Techniques	During various techniques of Breathing / Pranayama, you have to perform certain inhale & exhale techniques to improve per breathing cycle to 20, 30 seconds or more. More you hold your breath by Pranayama, it's good for a Yogi to increase life force, attain calm and quite state of mind.	Comparing other instruments, Flute has the additional advantage which takes Flute playing as close to meditation. To play, Flute, hold the breath for certain time say 15 – 20 seconds or more and side by side has to exhale the breath. After playing Raga on Flute, the flutist reaches that state of respiration cycle around 20 – 30 seconds or more per breath.
Objective of Dhyana	Please note that nature of mind is by default outward and to be specific to the external objects. The Objective of *Dhyana* in meditation is to fix your mind at certain position (*Kutastha* / Center of Eyebrows) inside our body. The purpose is to think inward and control the mind.	We recommend the Flute player to close the eyes and play from heart while playing for meditation. After certain period of playing, the player will observe a deep relaxation in body, mind and soul.

RIDDHI SANYAL

Interesting Parameters on Human Body	After practicing for 30 minutes of meditation, the respiration, heart rate, blood pressure will reduce and come under control. Ex: on Average: Respiration Rate: 2-3 in a minute Heart Rate: 65 - 70 / min or lesser Blood Pressure: 120/80 (can reduce 10 from the existing pressure of the person)	Same is the case of a flute player. After practicing 30 minutes of playing Raga in Base Flute (E), the similar phenomenon will be observed in the flute player. For meditating, we recommend the flutist to play the Ragas of type Peace, like playing Shuddha Kalyan at night. Ex: on Average: Respiration Rate: 3-4 in a minute Heart Rate: 60 - 70 / min Blood Pressure: Can reduce for high BP and come under control.
Inner Light / "Jyoti"	One of the Outcome of meditation is the person will get to see the reflection of inner light (*Jyoti*) with his pure and static mind. Once the mind is static, he/she can realize the life-force or existence of *Prana*.	If playing long time closing the eyes, there are chances that the player may get to see holy light in the center of eye-brows, that is the *Kutastha* or meditating point of self-realization. That gifts the same realization outcomes from meditation.
Ultimate Goal	Relaxation of Body and Mind. *Dhyana* on Center of Eyebrows / *Kutastha*. Self-Realization / feel the existence of life force / *Prana*.	We recommend the player to close the eyes and play from heart while playing for meditation. After certain period of playing, the player will observe a deep relaxation in body, mind and soul. Depending upon the concentration level, player may observe a very good *Dhyana* at *Kutastha*. Upon such real life experience, you are recommended to continue to concentrate on the *Dhyana*.

Table 15: Performing Meditation and Playing Raga in Flute - Observations

RIDDHI SANYAL

15.0   About Guruji, Musical Maestro Sri D. Madhusudan

Guruji's life and Guru Lineages

My Guruji, Sri D. Madhusudan is a famous Flutist from Uttarpara, Kolkata. His father was a direct disciple of **Pt. Gour Goswami**, a legendary flutist of Golden era time in Indian Music. Pt. Gour Goswami was direct disciple of Pt. Pannalal Ghosh. That's how we are connected to **Pt. Pannalal Ghosh** and to **Baba Allauddin Khan Saheb**.

Sri D. Madhusudan has taken his initial lessons from his father. Later on, he has taken advance lessons from **Sri. Chandrakanta Nandi**. After a stage of learning, **Sri Chandrakanta** send him to another teacher for advanced learning - **Sri Pranab Kumar Mukherjee**. Guruji's additionally plays 8-Hole Indian Clasical Flute in Scale E, that is the innovation, creation & teaching of **Sri Pranab Kumar Mukherjee**.

Guruji is a down to earth person. With simple explanations, he helps us to grow our knowledge both in Indian Classical Music & Western Music beyond the Musical Instruments. Every day practicing and self-corrections are key teachings. Without any ego Guruji often says, "*I am still constantly learning and practicing.*"

One small story on our Guruji will help you to realize his eagerness of learning. One day he was travelling in a bus to return home. On the way, he was able to listen to beautiful tune in Flute. On the next stoppage, he got down and walked back to the source of music. That was well ahead of his home. Once he arrived to the source of music, he found a boy playing Flute without any proper technique, but able to make excellent tune. Guruji has learned that tune from that boy. That boy was **Palash Taru Guha**, another popular Flutist of Bengal. That is how they became very good friends.

My First visit to Guruji

I can still remember very well on my first visit to Guruji. Rewinding back, now it feels that it was a pre-decided connection. Guruji went to Malda for a public function on 2010. He was presenting various Ragas like *Raga Puriya Kalyan*[14] in the Auditorium. My mother visited to listen there and she identified one of my brother's friend who is Guruji's disciple. That's how she made the connection first and informed me to come to Guruji's Kolkata class at Jadavpur.

When I reached there in the class in Jadavpur, he was teaching to various students. On my turn, he asked me to play anything. I played one *Bhatiali*[15] song - *Amay Dubaili*

---

[14] *Raga Puriya Kalyan or Puriya is an evening Raga with its close match to Yaman with Komal (Flat) Re. It belongs to Marwa Thaat.*

[15] *Bhatiali or bhatiyali is a form of folk music in both Bangladesh and West Bengal. Bhatiali is a river song mostly sung by boatmen while going down streams of the river. The word bhatiyali comes from bhata meaning downstream. "Amay Dubaili Re" is the famous Bhatiali song, which was sang by Manna Dey in the movie Ganga.*

RIDDHI SANYAL

Re. After listening and observing, he told that he would teach me. *"But you have to change the style and finger positions completely."* That is how I have started with flute.

Musical Experience of Guruji in various instruments

We have observed Guruji playing almost all possible instruments. By profession, he is a Flutist and Music Teacher. Following lines will touch his experience & versatility in different musical instruments –

String Instruments:

Guitar: When Guruji plays Guitar, it will look like he is a professional Guitarist. On playing classical, his lead guitar sounds like he is playing Sarod. While directing the program / function, he plays chord & lead in Guitar. *"Earlier days I have learned Hawaii Guitar. During those days in 70s & 80s, Hawaiian guitar was more played than Acoustic Guitar in Indian Music. Now it's all Acoustic Guitar with variance like 12 Stringer, Nylon String, etc".* We have observed his students playing classical in Nylon string guitar like a maestro. Guruji has taken his Guitar lessons from **Sri Nilratan Chandra** and **Sri Abhijit Paul**.

Mandolin: D. Madhusudan is one of the expert on playing Mandolin. Limited people are there in the music industry with the esthetic sense on where to sustain, how to provide filler music, how to play chord in Mandolin etc. We have observed Guruji playing Mandolin like a Maestro. His students' group (known as *Beniyasahakala*), has performed several Ragas, light music, Bollywood songs in Mandolin. *"Sometimes it's like 20 Mandolin players performing together."* – Rare in today's world. Many people from western world has requested to learn / play with D. Madhusudan while listening to different Ragas / light music in Mandolin orchestra.

Banjo: We have observed Guruji to play & teach Banjo professionally. He has applied Banjo in proper area in the orchestra where it suits. For example, application of Banjo is more on countryside music, folk music, northeastern *Bhatiali* music etc.

Sarod: When Guruji plays Sarod, it is our blessings to listen such vast application of the instrument. Apart from it's classical beauty, Sarod is applied in orchestra in proper esthetic sense where we have to mingle the String & Bowing instruments.

Bowing Instrument:

Flute: The term Bansuri / Flute reminds me to my Guruji always. He is the end-to-end complete Flutist. Starting from purchasing of Bamboo, creation of professional Flute, fine tuning of the Flutes, performing, teaching, demonstrating in workshop – we have seen him to do all of them. Some of his Professional performances are in youtube. The Raga *Ahir Bhairav*[16], is so much popular (over million views), that people have given feedback from all over world like *"Every morning we got up and listen to the*

---

[16] *Ahir Bhairav is a morning Raga on the Thaat Bhairav with the flavor of Kafi.*

RIDDHI SANYAL

Raga Ahir Bhairav by D. Madhusudan". Some other performances like Raga Chandrakauns[17], Raga Puriya Kalyan, Raga Desh etc are famous in youtube.

Violin, Cello: Observed Guruji to play Violin and the *Alaap* of the Raga will take you in a different mood. Professionally he teaches Violin to the students with both Western and Indian Raga style. Our violin orchestra depicts a picture of 10-15 violin players playing Ragas, light music etc. Interested and advanced Violin students get a chance to learn cello from Him.

Eshraz, Sarangi: These instruments are rare to observe nowadays, but you will still find that students are learning Eshraz and some are learning Sarangi. While playing in group / *Jugalbandi (Duet)*, the application of these instruments need specialized skills and esthetic sense to choose the suitable notes for Sarangi / Eshraz.

Composition, Direction & Complete Orchestra: Guruji has the experience in music direction since last 30-35 years. The group Beniyasahakala is formed 20 years back to play the orchestra music. Different musical instruments are performed on Classical, Semi-classical music, Western classical, Rabindra Sangeet, Nazrulgeeti, Bollywood & Tollywood songs, Patriotic songs etc.

Guruji has composed over 100 musical notations. We are lucky to get them for our learning, playing and participating in the orchestra with either stroke / bowing instruments. One of his famous composition is Istikutum – song of bird, which was first recorded in 2012 by 20 flutist. Some of his musical compositions are –

- Jhumur Gaan (in Folk Music, 2014)
- Arabian Tune (On tune from Middle East, 2016)
- Punjab Express (On Punjabi *Dhun*, 2012)
- Tandob Dance of Lord Shiva (On Malkauns Raga, 2012)
- Canada-Lady (On Raga Hansadhwani, 2016)
- *Bhatiali* Group Performance (On *Bhatiali* music, 2015)
- *Obastob* – Unrealistic (2017)
- Title Music (Performed as opening song, 2012)
- Focus (Based on Folk, 2014)
- Baisakhi (Based on Raga Salang Sarang, 2011)
- Violin Concert (On Raga Deshkar, 2016)
- Dumur (Based on Folk, 2014)
- March Music (On Western Marching music, 2013)
- Melancholy (on Raga Asavari, 2014)
- Last Fine Morning (Western, 2011)
- Miyan Mallar (On the Raga Miyan Mallar in Rupak, 2012)
- Shivaranjani (On the Raga Shivaranjani in Dadra, 2013)

---

[17] *Raga Chandrakauns belongs to Thaat Kafi and its best suited in night.*

RIDDHI SANYAL

16.0   Appendix

Topic	Details & Corresponding Western equivalent w.r.t scale C
Swar	Swar (Swara) is the Sanskrit / Hindi term of single Note.
Swaralipi	Swaralipi is the Sanskrit / Hindi term of Notation.
Sargam	In Brief, combination of SRGmPDNŜ are called Sargam. It's the small musical piece combination of the notes. Ex: SG RS Gm PN Ŝ NŜ NP mG RS
Shuddha	The 7 major notes SRGmPDN are termed as Shuddha Swars. Corresponding western notes are CDEFGAB
Komal (Flat) & Tibra (Sharp) notes	There are 4 Komal Swars / notes – Komal re, symbol r (C# / Db), Komal ga, symbol g (D# / Eb) Komal dha, symbol d (G# / Ab), Komal ni, symbol n (A# / Bb) There is only 1 Tibra Swar – Tibra Ma, symbol M (F# / Gb)
Higher Octave Symbols	Ŝ r̂ R̂ ĝ Ĝ ṁ Ṁ
Middle Octave Symbols	S r R g G m M P d D n N
Lower Octave Symbols	P̱ ḏ Ḏ ṉ Ṉ
Bol	A bol is a mnemonic syllable. It is used in Indian music to define the taal, or rhythmic pattern, and is one of the most important parts of Indian rhythm. Bol is derived from the Hindi word bolna, which means "to speak."
Rabindra Sangeet	Rabindra Sangeet, also known as Tagore Songs, are songs from the Indian subcontinent written and composed by the Bengali polymath, Greatest Poet, Rabindranath Tagore, winner of the 1913 Nobel Prize in Literature. Tagore was a prolific composer with around 2,230 songs to his credit. The songs have distinctive characteristics in the music of Bengal, popular in India and Bangladesh.
Vadi & Samavadi	Vadi, is the most important / tonic (root) *swara* / note of the Raga. Samvadi is the 2nd important note of the Raga after Vadi.
Taan	Taan is the area of Raga to generate the mood (Bhava) of the Raga. You can play any number of Taan till the mood is sustained. If the beat of the Taal is 16 (say Tintaal), Taan can be played in beats of 8, 16, 24, 32 and so on.
Tihai	When same notes are repeated 3 times, it's called Tihai. This beautifies the representation of the Raga when it matches to the Som (+) or Phak (0) position of the Taal.

RIDDHI SANYAL

Gat (Sthai / Bandish), Antara	Bandish or Gat (also called Sthai) is the first two lines of the Raga with the Taal. The next section or verse is called Antara. That is typically line number 3 & 4. These four lines can be played as-is during the initial days of practice.

17.0   Index

Figures

Figure 1: Default Flute sound. Tibra Ma - Notation symbol M. (F# w.r.t. C Scale)__ 13

Figure 2: Flute position - Ma - Notation symbol m. (F w.r.t. C Scale) _____ 14

Figure 3: Flute position - Ga - Notation symbol G. (E w.r.t. C Scale)_____ 15

Figure 4: Flute position - Re - Notation symbol R. (D w.r.t. C Scale)_____ 16

Figure 5: Flute position - Sa - Notation symbol S. (C w.r.t. C Scale) _____ 17

Figure 6: Flute position - Pa - Notation symbol P. (G w.r.t. C Scale)_____ 18

Figure 7: Flute position - Dha - Notation symbol D. (A w.r.t. C Scale)_____ 19

Figure 8: Flute position - Ni - Notation symbol N. (B w.r.t. C Scale) _____ 20

Figure 9: Flute position - Sa' - Notation symbol Ŝ. (C6 w.r.t. C5 Scale) _____ 21

Figure 10: Flute position - Ni - Notation symbol N. (B4 w.r.t. C5 Scale) _____ 21

Figure 11: Flute position - Dha - Notation symbol D. (A4 w.r.t. C5 Scale) _____ 22

Figure 12: Flute position - Pa - Notation symbol P. (G4 w.r.t. C5 Scale)_____ 22

Figure 13: Flute position – Re' - Notation symbol R̂. (D6 w.r.t. C6 Scale)_____ 22

Figure 14: Flute position – Ga' - Notation symbol Ĝ. (E6 w.r.t. C5 Scale)_____ 23

Figure 15: Flute position - Ma' - Notation symbol ṁ. (F6 w.r.t. C5 Scale) _____ 23

Figure 16: Flute position - ni - Notation symbol n. (Bb w.r.t. C Scale)_____ 41

Tables

Table 1: Lower Octave - Indian Notation, Western Notation and Flute Hole position 9

Table 2: Middle Octave - Indian Notation, Western Notation and Flute Hole position
.... 10

Table 3: Higher Octave - Indian Notation, Western Notation and Flute Hole position
.... 10

Table 4: Indian Taal (Rhythms) with common Bol / Strokes 29

Table 5: Raga Hansadhwani – Upward direction / Arohana 60

RIDDHI SANYAL

Table 6: Raga Hansadhwani – Downward direction / Avarohana 60

Table 7: Raga Durga – Upward direction / Arohana 67

Table 8: Raga Durga – Downward direction / Avarohana 67

Table 9: Raga Bilaval – Upward direction / Arohana 72

Table 10: Raga Bilaval – Downward direction / Avarohana 72

Table 11: Raga Mand – Upward direction / Arohana 76

Table 12: Raga Mand – Downward direction / Avarohana 76

Table 13: Raga Bhupali – Upward direction / Arohana 81

Table 14: Raga Bhupali – Downward direction / Avarohana 81

Table 15: Performing Meditation and Playing Raga in Flute - Observations 102

Exercises

Exercise 1: Play 2 same notes at a time 24

Exercise 2: Play 2 sequential notes at a time 26

Exercise 3: Play alternate notes 27

Exercise 4: Play Notes with 8 Beat Rhythm (Keherwa Tal) 30

Exercise 5A: Play Notes with Whole Rests – Indian Notation 31

Exercise 6: Play ½ Notes with 1/2 Rests – Indian Notation 33

Exercise 7: Learn 6 Beat – Indian Convention 34

Exercise 8: Play 3 notes at a time – Indian Convention 35

Exercise 9: Play 4 notes at a time – Indian Convention 36

Exercise 10: Learn 6 Beat – Indian Convention 37

Exercise 11: Revision & Additional Exercise – Indian Convention 39

Exercise 12: Play Happy Birthday – Indian Convention 41

Exercise 13: Play 'Twinkle Twinkle' – Indian Convention 42

Exercise 14: Play 'We Shall Overcome' – Indian Convention 43

Exercise 15: Play 'Jamaican Farewell' – Indian Convention 45

Exercise 16: Play 'DO A DEER' – Indian Convention 47

Exercise 17: Play 'Auld Lang Syne' – Indian Convention 49

Exercise 18: Play 'A Chal Ke Tujhe' – Indian Convention 51

Exercise 19: Play 'Phule Phule – Flowers – Rabindra Sangeet' – Indian Convention. 53

Exercise 20: Play 'Om Jai Jagadish Hare' – Indian Convention 55

Exercise 21: Play 'Closing Ceremony Harmony Music' 58

RIDDHI SANYAL

Exercise 22: Raga Hansadhwani - Alaap..61

Exercise 23: Raga Hansadwani (Shorter notation) – Indian Convention 62

Exercise 24: Raga Hansadhwani (Elaborated notation) – Indian Convention...........64

Exercise 25: Raga Durga - Alaap..68

Exercise 26: Raga Durga – Indian Convention 68

Exercise 27: Rag Bilaval - Alaap..73

Exercise 28: Rag Bilaval - Indian Convention 73

Exercise 29: Rag Mand - Alaap 76

Exercise 30: Raga Mand – Indian Convention..77

Exercise 31: Rag Bhupali - Alaap...81

Exercise 32: Raga Bhupali – Indian Convention 82

Sheet Music

Sheet Music 1: Play 2 Same Notes at a time...25

Sheet Music 2: Play 2 Sequential Notes at a time..27

Sheet Music 3: Play Alternative Notes 28

Sheet Music 4: Play Notes with 4/4 beats...30

Sheet Music 5: Learn Rest / Gap for Whole, Half, Quarter and Eighth Gaps 32

Sheet Music 6: Play Eighth Notes and Rests 33

Sheet Music 7: Customized exercise for Flute practice 34

Sheet Music 8: Play Progression on 3 Notes in 6 beats (3/4).............................35

Sheet Music 9: Play Progression on 4 Notes in 8 beats (4/4)............................36

Sheet Music 10: Play Notes on 6 beats (3/4) in Dadra Taal...............................38

Sheet Music 11: Revision exercise for Flute on 8 beat 40

Sheet Music 12: Play Happy Birthday 42

Sheet Music 13: Play 'Twinkle Twinkle'...43

Sheet Music 14: Play 'We Shall Overcome'..44

Sheet Music 15: Play Jamaican Farewell 46

Sheet Music 16: Play 'Do A Deer a Female Deer'...48

Sheet Music 17: Play 'Auld Lang Syne'..50

Sheet Music 18: Play Hindi song tune 'A Chal Ke Tujhe' 52

Sheet Music 19: Play 'Phule Phule' 54

Sheet Music 20: Play 'Om Jai Jagadish Hare'...57

RIDDHI SANYAL

Sheet Music 21: 'Closing Ceremony Harmony Music' 59

Sheet Music 22: Raga Hansadhwani - Western Convention Page 1 65

Sheet Music 23: Raga Hansadhwani - Western Convention Page 2 66

Sheet Music 24: Raga Durga – Western Convention, Page 1 70

Sheet Music 25: Raga Durga – Western Convention, Page 2 71

Sheet Music 26: Raga Durga – Western Convention, Page 3 72

Sheet Music 27: Rag Bilaval - Western Convention, Page 1 74

Sheet Music 28: Rag Bilaval - Western Convention, Page 2 75

Sheet Music 29: Raga Mand – Western Convention, Page 1 78

Sheet Music 30: Raga Mand – Western Convention, Page 2 79

Sheet Music 31: Raga Mand – Western Convention, Page 3 80

Sheet Music 32: Raga Bhupali – Western Convention, Page 1 83

Sheet Music 33: Raga Bhupali – Western Convention, Page 2 84

Sheet Music 34: Raga Bhupali – Western Convention, Page 3 85

18.0   References

1. Pt Pannalal Ghosh *Retrieved from* https://en.wikipedia.org/wiki/Pannalal_Ghosh
2. Raga / Raag, Ragam, Ragini *Retrieved from* *https://en.wikipedia.org/wiki/Raga*
3. List of Ragas *Retrieved from*
   https://en.wikipedia.org/wiki/List_of_Ragas_in_Hindustani_classical_music
4. Pt Hari Prashad Chaurasia *Retrieved from*
   https://en.wikipedia.org/wiki/Hariprasad_Chaurasia
5. Beat (Music) *Retrieved from* https://en.wikipedia.org/wiki/Beat_(music)
6. Taal / Tala (Music) *Retrieved from* *https://en.wikipedia.org/wiki/Tala_(music)*
7. Auld Lang Syne *Retrieved from* https://en.wikipedia.org/wiki/Auld_Lang_Syne
8. Raga Hansadhwani *Retrieved from* *https://en.wikipedia.org/wiki/Hamsadhvani*
9. Raga Durga *Retrieved from* *https://en.wikipedia.org/wiki/Durga_(raga)*
10. Indian Music Notations Received from
    https://en.wikipedia.org/wiki/Vishnu_Narayan_Bhatkhande
11. Bhatiali Received from https://en.wikipedia.org/wiki/Bhatiali
12. Rabindra Sangeet *Retrieved from* *https://en.wikipedia.org/wiki/Rabindra_Sangeet*

19.0   About the Author

Riddhi has been in the music industry for more than 20 years. His musical journey starts from childhood. His mother, *Smt. Gargi Sanyal* is a well-known *Rabindra Sangeet* singer and learnt from Legendary *Suchitra Mitra* at Rabithirtha. Grandmother, *Smt Tripti Saraswati* was a classical singer and had taken coaching to *Pt. Jamini Ganguly* and Legendary *Sri Manabendra Mukherjee*. Sister, *Smt Madhupa Sanyal* is vocalist and had learnt advanced lessons from *Pt. Ajay Chakraborty* at Shrutinandan. Musical culture is there at home since childhood. Musical gathering (*Ganer Ashor*) is very much common at home and sometimes everyone is deeply tuned into music, that even time passes from evening to late night on those homely musical occasions.

During childhood, Riddhi has learn Tabla from famous teacher **Sri Abhijit Barhouri** at Malda. During those days, famous singer & Harmonium maestro, **Sri Alok Bhadhury**, used to come at our home at teach music. During his college life, Riddhi has started to learn Flute from his friend **Sri Sajal Banerjee**. That flute was metallic and holding technique was similar to Shehnai. Later on Riddhi has learned to play the Bamboo flute by self-practicing and performed in the college functions.

During staying at USA (2007 – 2010), studying at various library at Minneapolis, he has learnt sheet music. He has performed at US, at the **Minneapolis during Durga Puja festival** organized by BAM. There he has played *Rabindra Sangeet* and North Eastern *Bhatiali* Music. Everyone has appreciated with the type of music and especially on Larger Flute (F#) they have first time observed at US. Feedback he received after function – "*It's rare to have Indian flute / Bansuri in the US functions and it was awesome to listen to the Indian & North Eastern tunes*". His wife Priyanka had accompanied on that function with Keyboard.

Finally, he has made with musical Guruji, **Sri D. Madhusudan** at Jadavpur class during 2010. Since then it is all Guruji's guidance. Riddhi has performed classical music, Raga, Light classical music, Rabindra Sangeet, Bollywood Golden Era songs, Patriotic songs etc. on Flute & Harmonica in lot of places - During Durga Puja, Diwali & Maa Kali Puja at Kolkata, Uttarpara, Malda, Dasaswamedh Ghat, Varanasi, Function at Bangalore, Mangalore, etc.

By profession, Riddhi is Sr. Architect in one of the largest Software Company. Staying in IT industry for 17 years, he has never stopped practicing or teaching music. He has performed in front of several customer visits and corporate functions. Once he had played Raga Hansadhwani on Flute to the CIO & Board of directors of one of the largest Travel Company. He eyes were perplexed and he was like overwhelmed during the entire duration of concert. At the end, he told that, until now he has listened to this kind of concert in TV. First time he has seen someone playing in front of him and he has no words to explain the sensation.

RIDDHI SANYAL

20.0   Feedback & Contacts

This book is designed in such a way that, readers across the world will be able to start in Flute / Bansuri and gain interest in Classical Music. Step by step guidance is provided on holding the flute, first time blowing, playing the preliminary notes in multiple octaves, playing with beats & rhythm, learning to play various songs, *Bhajans* and finally learning the classical ragas in Flute. There is no age barrier to start on the learnings. Golden time with Musical Maestros picturizes of life of musicians & composers. The Flute & Meditation section enters the world of positive vibes.

You can share your review & rating and get in touch at any social media of your choice. Upon your feedback, next version can be improvised.

Email: Riddhi.Sanyal@gmail.com

Phone Number: +91 9051653871

WhatsApp: https://wa.me/919051653871

YouTube Channel: https://www.youtube.com/c/MusicalJourneys

Instagram: https://www.instagram.com/riddhi.sanyal/

Facebook Profile: https://www.facebook.com/riddhi.sanyal.12

Author Page: https://www.amazon.com/author/riddhi

Printed in Great Britain
by Amazon